Step Up to Success: A Beginner's Guide to Starting a Flooring Business

Introduction

Welcome to *Step Up to Success: A Beginner's Guide to Starting a Flooring Business.* If you've ever considered entering the flooring industry and creating a profitable, rewarding business, you're in the right place. The flooring business is more than just about providing surfaces to walk on—it's about creating spaces, delivering quality, and enhancing the everyday environments of homes and businesses.

This guide is designed with beginners in mind. Whether you're a tradesperson looking to branch out on your own, an entrepreneur exploring a new field, or someone with a passion for interiors, this book will take you step-by-step through the foundational aspects of launching and growing a successful flooring business. Flooring is a versatile, competitive industry, but with the right approach, your business can thrive by offering something unique and valuable to clients.

What You'll Find in This Book

Throughout this guide, we'll cover the essential steps for establishing your business, from crafting a clear business plan and securing the necessary licenses to understanding the types of flooring materials, managing projects efficiently, and building a loyal client base. Each chapter is crafted to give you practical insights and strategies to help you navigate the challenges and seize the opportunities that come with running a flooring business.

Why Flooring?

The flooring industry is an attractive choice for new business owners because it combines skilled craftsmanship with entrepreneurial opportunity. Flooring businesses offer essential services that are always in demand—whether for new construction, remodeling, or repair. It's a field where high-quality work and exceptional customer service can set your business apart, building a reputation that leads to growth and sustainability.

The Goal of This Guide

Starting a business is challenging, but our goal is to break down the process into actionable steps that make the journey manageable and achievable. In each chapter, you'll gain knowledge not only about setting up your business but also about creating a brand that resonates with clients, managing projects efficiently, handling finances smartly, and adapting to industry trends. By the end of this book, you'll have a solid understanding of what it takes to succeed in the flooring industry, ready to face the challenges of entrepreneurship with confidence.

So, if you're ready to "step up" to the challenge and lay the foundation for a business built on quality, service, and resilience, let's get started. Together, we'll turn your vision into a reality and help you create a flooring business that stands the test of time.

Step Up to Success: A Beginner's Guide to Starting a Flooring Business

Introduction

Chapter 1: Understanding the Flooring Industry Landscape

Chapter 2: Setting Up Your Business for Success

Chapter 3: Knowing Your Products – Types of Flooring Materials

Chapter 4: Marketing Your Flooring Business for Growth

Chapter 5: Building Customer Relationships for Long-Term Success

Chapter 6: Managing Finances for a Thriving Business

Chapter 7: Building a Strong Team

Chapter 8: Navigating Challenges and Building Resilience

Chapter 9: Dealing with Competition in the Flooring Business

Chapter 10: Looking Ahead to Continued Success

Chapter 1: Understanding the Flooring Industry Landscape

Getting to Know the Flooring Industry

The flooring industry might seem straightforward at first glance, but it's a dynamic sector filled with opportunities, choices, and specialized knowledge. For those just starting, understanding the big picture and the various types of flooring businesses is crucial. This chapter is designed to give you that foundation so you can approach your new business with insight and clarity.

The flooring industry covers more than just installing carpets or laying hardwood. It's about enhancing spaces and creating environments that reflect personal style and functionality. Flooring professionals help clients make significant decisions, guiding them through the maze of materials, costs, and aesthetics. As a business owner, you'll not only be a product expert but also an advisor, salesperson, and skilled strategist.

Why Start a Flooring Business Now?

The timing for starting a flooring business couldn't be better. With more people investing in home renovations and commercial spaces adapting to new standards, flooring has become a focal point of design. The global flooring market is expected to grow steadily, driven by rising urbanization, construction projects, and increasing preferences for stylish and sustainable interiors.

The Opportunity in Flooring
Starting a business in this field offers flexibility. You might choose to specialize in certain flooring types, such as eco-friendly bamboo or durable vinyl for high-traffic areas. Or perhaps you'll focus on a specific market—residential homes, commercial spaces, or restoration work. Whatever path you choose, remember that your business is more than just flooring; it's about enhancing lives and spaces.

Types of Flooring Businesses: Finding Your Niche

To succeed, it's essential to define your business type and niche. There are several models, each with its own pros and cons:

1. Retail Flooring Business

A retail flooring business sells flooring materials directly to customers. This model requires substantial knowledge of materials and styles, as well as good supplier relationships. You'll help customers choose products, offering samples, information, and possibly design advice.

2. Installation-Only Business

Some flooring businesses focus solely on installation. If you have strong technical skills and want to avoid managing inventory, this could be a good fit. An installation-focused business requires skilled staff and equipment for handling various materials.

3. Full-Service Flooring Business

This model combines both retail and installation. Offering a complete package can attract customers who appreciate the convenience of a one-stop shop. A full-service flooring business usually has higher startup costs, as you'll manage both inventory and service teams.

4. Restoration and Refinishing Services

Specializing in restoration can be a niche yet profitable area. Many clients look to restore original wood floors or upgrade aging materials, and providing refinishing services can help you stand out. This model typically requires specialized equipment and skilled artisans.

5. Consulting and Design Service

Some businesses focus solely on consulting and design, helping clients choose materials, plan layouts, and budget for projects. This model works well if you have an eye for design and enjoy working with clients on a more advisory basis.

Understanding these options will help you decide where to focus. Take the time to research your local market and assess which services are most in demand. Your initial choice will set the tone for your brand and customer interactions.

Key Market Trends and Customer Needs

In any industry, understanding current trends and customer needs is essential for success. Flooring is no exception. As a new business owner, being aware of industry shifts will not only help you position your brand effectively but also enable you to provide products and services that truly resonate with your target audience.

The flooring market today is shaped by trends that reflect changes in both customer expectations and technological advancements. From the types of materials customers prefer to the ways they expect their flooring to be installed, these trends will guide your approach and help you stay ahead in a competitive market.

Trend 1: Sustainability and Eco-Friendly Materials

One of the most influential trends in the flooring industry is the rising demand for sustainable, eco-friendly materials. Today's consumers are more conscious than ever about the impact of their purchases on the environment, and this awareness extends to flooring. Materials like bamboo, cork, and reclaimed wood are popular for their sustainability. In addition, there's a growing interest in flooring products with lower volatile organic compound (VOC) emissions, which contribute to indoor air quality.

For your business, offering eco-friendly flooring options can set you apart from competitors who only provide conventional materials. You may want to emphasize these products in your marketing and educate customers on the benefits of choosing green flooring options.

Trend 2: Durability and Easy Maintenance

Durability and easy maintenance are increasingly becoming top priorities for flooring buyers, especially in high-traffic areas like commercial spaces or busy households. Customers want materials that withstand heavy use, require minimal upkeep, and maintain their appearance over time. Vinyl plank and luxury vinyl tile (LVT), for instance, have gained popularity because they're resilient, water-resistant, and easy to clean.

As a business owner, staying informed about these durable materials and educating clients about their benefits can enhance your reputation as a knowledgeable provider. Clients appreciate recommendations that consider both aesthetic appeal and practicality.

Trend 3: Customization and Unique Styles

Today's customers desire unique, personalized spaces, which has led to a growing demand for customized flooring solutions. Homeowners and businesses alike are looking for ways to make their floors stand out, whether through intricate patterns, bold colors, or unusual textures. Techniques like parquet flooring, herringbone patterns, and mixed materials allow clients to express their style.

Offering customization options can help differentiate your business from others. If feasible, partner with suppliers or artisans who can provide unique styles, textures, or patterns, and consider building a portfolio of completed projects to inspire potential customers.

Trend 4: Technological Advancements in Installation

In recent years, technology has made flooring installation more efficient and precise. Innovations in adhesives, subfloor preparation, and modular flooring options have transformed the process, saving time and reducing labor costs. Some businesses are investing in tools like laser measurement devices and automated installation systems to streamline the process further.

For a new business, investing in technology-enhanced tools may be beneficial in the long run, allowing your team to work efficiently and provide a better customer experience. Efficient installations lead to satisfied clients, positive reviews, and potential referrals.

Trend 5: Health and Wellness Considerations

Alongside sustainability, there's a heightened focus on health and wellness in the building and renovation industries. Flooring choices impact indoor air quality, noise levels, and even slip resistance, making it crucial to offer products that support a healthy environment. Hypoallergenic carpets, low-VOC vinyl, and non-slip surfaces are some of the features that appeal to health-conscious clients.

Educating customers on the health benefits of different flooring options can make your business stand out as one that cares about client well-being. It's a powerful way to build trust, especially among families, healthcare facilities, and wellness-oriented commercial spaces.

Assessing the Competition

Understanding your competition is a critical step in building a successful flooring business. By analyzing your competitors, you can identify gaps in the market, discover potential opportunities, and avoid common pitfalls. This section will guide you through practical steps for assessing your competition and using that insight to shape your business strategy.

Why Analyze Competitors?

When you first enter the flooring industry, knowing what other companies are doing can provide valuable insight into customer expectations and service standards. Observing competitors allows you to set realistic goals, refine your offerings, and avoid mistakes. Here are some reasons why competitor analysis is essential:

1. Identify Service Gaps: By studying your competitors' offerings, you may spot services that are underrepresented in the market, such as high-quality installation, eco-friendly options, or budget-friendly services.

2. Set Competitive Prices: Understanding your competitors' pricing can help you develop a pricing model that is attractive to customers while maintaining profitability. This is especially useful if you're operating in a

highly competitive market.

3. Gain Insight on Customer Preferences: Reading customer reviews and testimonials for other flooring businesses can reveal which services customers appreciate most—and which areas competitors might be lacking in.

4. Enhance Your Marketing Strategy: By observing competitors' marketing techniques, you can see which methods seem effective and where you might differentiate yourself.

Steps to Conduct Competitor Analysis

1. List Your Competitors
   Start by listing local flooring businesses, both big and small, that operate in your area. Include retail stores, installation companies, and any specialized flooring services that might overlap with your target market.

2. Research Their Offerings and Specializations
   Visit their websites, social media pages, and online listings to get a sense of their product range, installation services, and specializations. Take note of what materials they focus on, whether they offer eco-friendly options, and if they specialize in certain types of flooring.

3. Study Their Pricing Model
   While exact pricing details might not be readily available, many businesses publish starting prices or offer quotes upon request. Take the time to gather as much information as possible to understand where their services fall in the pricing spectrum.

4. Read Customer Reviews
   Platforms like Google, Yelp, and Angie's List can be gold mines for insights into a competitor's strengths and weaknesses. Pay attention to common themes in reviews—whether positive or negative—as they indicate areas where you might exceed customer expectations.

5. Observe Their Marketing Techniques

Competitors' websites, social media profiles, and advertisements provide clues about their marketing approach. Look for unique selling points (USPs), promotional tactics, and the tone of their messaging. This can inspire ideas for how you might position your brand differently.

6. Visit Their Showroom or Store

If possible, visit competitors' showrooms or stores to get a firsthand look at their operations. Observe their staff's expertise, how they handle customer interactions, and how the space is set up. This can give you ideas for creating a memorable customer experience in your own business.

Using Competitor Insights to Strengthen Your Business

Once you've gathered information about your competitors, it's time to put those insights to work. Here's how:

- Differentiate Your Brand: Think about what makes your business unique. If competitors lack eco-friendly options, for example, you might focus on a green flooring initiative. If their customer service receives criticism, make quality service a pillar of your brand.

- Optimize Your Service Offerings: Use what you've learned to refine your services. If customers consistently mention long wait times for installations, you could highlight fast and reliable scheduling as part of your offering.

- Set Competitive Prices Wisely: With an understanding of the pricing landscape, position your pricing to appeal to your target audience. If you're offering premium products, make sure your branding and customer experience reflect the value.

- Develop a Unique Marketing Strategy: Avoid copying competitors' strategies directly. Instead, use your insights to create a distinctive marketing approach that highlights your business's strengths.

Remember, competitor analysis is not a one-time task. Regularly reviewing your competitors will help you stay agile in a changing market, adapt to new trends, and continuously improve your services.

Identifying Your Unique Selling Proposition (USP)

One of the most important steps in building a successful flooring business is defining your Unique Selling Proposition, or USP. A USP is what sets your business apart from the competition, making it clear to customers why they should choose you over others. In an industry with diverse offerings, a strong USP can make all the difference, helping you attract clients, build loyalty, and ultimately grow your business.

What Is a USP, and Why Does It Matter?

Your USP is a promise you make to your customers. It's the answer to their question, "Why should I choose this business?" A strong USP isn't just about being different; it's about being meaningfully different in a way that appeals directly to your target market. Here's why a compelling USP is crucial for a new business:

1. It Grabs Attention: In a crowded market, a clear and unique message can cut through the noise, helping potential customers notice your brand.
2. It Builds Trust: A USP that focuses on quality, service, or specific expertise makes customers feel confident in choosing you.
3. It Guides Business Decisions: Your USP can shape your branding, marketing, and service approach, keeping you focused on what matters most to your clients.

Steps to Define Your USP

1. Identify Your Target Market's Needs
   Think about the primary needs and preferences of your target market. For instance, are they homeowners looking for budget-friendly solutions, or are they high-end clients interested in sustainable flooring options? A

good USP addresses the core desires and pain points of your audience.

2. Analyze Your Strengths

Consider what you bring to the table that competitors don't. Are you exceptionally knowledgeable about eco-friendly materials? Do you provide a streamlined, quick installation service that meets tight schedules? Your unique strengths should form the basis of your USP.

3. Study Competitor Gaps

In your competitor analysis, you may have identified areas where others fall short. For example, if many local businesses offer limited customization, you could position yourself as a flexible, design-driven provider.

4. Make It Clear and Concise

Your USP should be a single, clear sentence or statement. It doesn't have to cover everything you do—just the most compelling reason why clients should choose your business. For example, "We provide sustainable flooring solutions with a commitment to quality and eco-friendly practices."

5. Test Your USP with Feedback

Before finalizing your USP, share it with a few trusted individuals or potential customers for feedback. This can help ensure it resonates with the audience you're aiming to attract.

Examples of Strong USPs in the Flooring Industry

To better understand what an effective USP looks like, here are a few examples that address specific customer needs and set businesses apart:

- Eco-Conscious Flooring Solutions: "Helping you create beautiful, sustainable spaces with eco-friendly flooring that doesn't compromise on style or quality."
- Budget-Friendly Flooring for Busy Families: "Affordable, durable flooring solutions designed to withstand the wear and tear of family life—without breaking the bank."
- Luxury Custom Flooring for Distinctive Spaces: "Offering luxury

flooring with exclusive materials and custom designs to elevate your home or commercial space."

- Express Installation Service for Tight Deadlines: "When time is of the essence, we deliver professional, efficient installations that meet your schedule and exceed expectations."

Bringing Your USP to Life in Every Customer Interaction

Once you've defined your USP, it's time to integrate it into every aspect of your business. Your USP should not only be evident in your marketing but also in the way you interact with customers. Here are a few ways to make your USP a core part of your business operations:

- Marketing and Advertising: Use your USP in all marketing materials, from your website to social media profiles and brochures. This ensures that potential customers are introduced to your business with a clear sense of what you offer.
- Customer Service and Sales Approach: Train your team to emphasize your USP in customer interactions, making sure that every conversation reinforces the unique value you provide.
- Quality Control and Service Delivery: Make sure that your USP is reflected in your service delivery. For example, if your USP is fast installation, ensure your scheduling and work processes are streamlined for efficiency.
- Customer Feedback and Improvement: Regularly gather feedback to ensure that your business continues to deliver on its promise. Use any insights to adjust and enhance your services, ensuring that your USP remains relevant and valuable.

Your USP is the foundation upon which your brand identity is built. Defining and consistently delivering on it will help you establish a reputation, attract loyal customers, and stand out in the flooring industry.

Building a Brand That Resonates

Branding is more than just a logo or catchy slogan; it's the impression your business leaves on customers. In the flooring industry, a strong brand can mean the difference between being just another company and becoming a trusted, memorable name. This section will guide you through the basics of building a brand that resonates with your target audience and communicates your unique value.

The Elements of a Strong Brand

To create a successful brand, think of it as a blend of visuals, values, and promises that shape how people perceive your business. Here are some core elements of branding to consider:

1. Brand Name and Logo
   Your brand name should be memorable, easy to pronounce, and relevant to the services you offer. A logo is equally important as it acts as a visual anchor for your brand. Ensure that it's clean, professional, and versatile enough for various applications, from business cards to trucks.

2. Tagline or Slogan
   A short, impactful tagline can help reinforce your brand message. Think of it as a quick way to convey what sets you apart. For instance, if your USP is about quick and quality installations, your tagline might be, "Fast Floors, Lasting Quality."

3. Color Scheme and Design Style
   Your color scheme and overall design style should reflect the personality of your brand. Bright, bold colors can evoke energy and creativity, while neutral tones might communicate trust and professionalism. Consistent use of colors and fonts across your materials will help establish a cohesive look.

4. Brand Voice and Messaging
   Your brand voice is the tone and style in which you communicate with customers. Are you professional and knowledgeable, friendly and

approachable, or a mix of both? Your voice should reflect your values and appeal to your target audience. For example, a friendly, encouraging tone might resonate with residential customers, while a more formal voice could appeal to commercial clients.

Creating a Brand Story

A brand story adds depth to your business, helping potential customers feel connected to your journey. It should convey why you started the business, what motivates you, and the values that guide your services. When customers know the story behind your brand, they're more likely to feel a personal connection and remember your business.

Here's an example of a brand story:
"After working in the flooring industry for over a decade, I realized that many businesses focused on profits over people. I wanted to change that by creating a flooring company that prioritizes customer satisfaction, quality work, and eco-friendly practices. Today, we help families and businesses find flooring solutions that are not only beautiful but built to last."

Connecting Your Brand to Your USP

Your USP and brand go hand in hand. Use your USP as a focal point in your branding strategy. For instance, if your USP is centered around sustainability, let that value shine in your branding. Use green and earthy tones, feature eco-friendly icons, and include messaging that emphasizes your commitment to the environment. This consistency between your USP and brand image helps reinforce what makes your business unique.

Building Trust with Consistent Branding

One of the most powerful aspects of branding is consistency. When your brand identity is applied consistently across all touchpoints—your website, social media, print materials, uniforms, and even the tone of your communications—it fosters trust. Customers are more likely to choose a brand that feels familiar and reliable.

Here are a few areas where consistent branding can help you build trust:

- Website: Make sure your website aligns with your brand's colors, voice, and values. A well-designed site builds credibility and allows customers to get a feel for your business.
- Social Media: Social platforms are ideal for sharing your brand's personality. Post photos of your projects, customer testimonials, and tips to keep your audience engaged and reinforce your brand values.
- Customer Experience: Every interaction a customer has with your team should reflect your brand values. Whether they're calling to ask a question or visiting your store, consistent and positive experiences create lasting impressions.

Tips for Strengthening Your Brand Over Time

Branding is not a one-time task; it's something you can evolve as your business grows. Here are some tips to keep your brand strong and adaptable:

- Listen to Customer Feedback: Pay attention to what customers love about your brand and where you might improve. Adapting to feedback can help keep your brand relevant and customer-focused.
- Keep an Eye on Competitors: Regularly review competitors to ensure that your branding remains distinctive and aligned with your USP.
- Invest in Quality Marketing Materials: From business cards to brochures, quality materials reflect a professional image. As your business grows, consider refreshing your brand visuals to reflect the evolution of your company.

A strong brand helps build a loyal customer base, establishes trust, and makes your business memorable. With a well-defined brand, your flooring company will be set to stand out in the marketplace, capturing the attention of customers who value quality, trust, and expertise.

This completes Chapter 1 on understanding the flooring industry landscape!

Chapter 2: Setting Up Your Business for Success

Essential Steps to Register Your Flooring Business

Starting a flooring business requires more than just passion and knowledge about flooring. To build a legitimate and successful business, you'll need to go through essential legal steps to register your company. This process ensures you're compliant with local laws and can operate smoothly. In this chapter, we'll guide you through setting up the legal and structural foundations for your new business.

Step 1: Choosing a Business Structure

One of the first and most important decisions you'll make is choosing the legal structure of your business. The structure you choose will impact everything from your taxes and liability to how you operate and grow. Here are some common options:

1. Sole Proprietorship

A sole proprietorship is the simplest structure, ideal for those who want to run the business on their own. However, it doesn't offer any legal separation between your personal and business assets, which means you're personally liable for the business's debts and obligations.

2. Limited Liability Company (LLC)

An LLC provides a balance between flexibility and liability protection. It protects your personal assets in case of business liabilities or debts, making it a popular choice for small businesses. It also offers pass-through taxation, where the business income is taxed once, on your personal income.

3. Partnership

If you're planning to start the business with one or more partners, a partnership structure may be suitable. Like sole proprietorships, partnerships offer simplicity but require a clear agreement between partners. A limited liability partnership (LLP) can provide additional protection from personal liability.

4. Corporation

Corporations are separate legal entities from their owners, providing significant liability protection. However, they are more complex to manage and can be subject to double taxation. Corporations are generally recommended for larger businesses or those planning to raise substantial capital.

Step 2: Registering Your Business Name

Once you've chosen a business structure, it's time to register your business name. Your business name is often the first impression customers have, so choose a name that is memorable, reflects your brand, and clearly identifies your services.

1. Check Name Availability
   Start by ensuring that your chosen name is available. You can usually do this through your state's business registration portal. Check for both business name availability and domain name availability, as having a matching website domain will be beneficial.

2. File a Doing Business As (DBA) Name, If Necessary
   If you're operating under a different name than your legal business name, you may need to file a DBA (Doing Business As) with your local or state government. This allows you to use a brand name different from your registered company name.

3. Trademark Your Business Name (Optional)
   If you're planning to build a recognizable brand, consider trademarking your business name to protect it from being used by others in the industry. A trademark can give you exclusive rights to use your brand name and logo.

Step 3: Obtaining Necessary Licenses and Permits

The flooring industry often requires specific licenses and permits, which can vary by location. Some regions require contractor licenses for flooring installation, while others might require general business licenses. Be sure to check your local, state, and federal requirements to ensure compliance.

1. General Business License
   Most businesses require a general business license to operate legally. This can often be obtained through your city or county government.

2. Contractor's License
   If you'll be offering installation services, you may need a contractor's license. Requirements for a contractor's license vary widely, so check with your state's contractor licensing board.

3. Sales Tax Permit

If you're selling flooring materials directly to customers, you'll likely need a sales tax permit. This allows you to collect sales tax from customers and submit it to your state government.

4. Other Permits

Depending on your location and services, you may need additional permits. For example, if you plan to store large quantities of materials, you may need a fire department inspection or environmental permits.

Step 4: Setting Up a Business Bank Account

Once you're registered, it's essential to keep your finances separate from your personal accounts. Open a dedicated business bank account to help manage cash flow, track expenses, and simplify tax filing. Many banks offer small business accounts with benefits such as cash management tools and lower fees.

1. Prepare Required Documentation

When opening a business account, you'll usually need documents such as your business registration certificate, EIN (Employer Identification Number), and personal identification.

2. Consider a Business Credit Card

A business credit card can help you build credit for your company, manage cash flow, and earn rewards on your purchases. Be sure to use the card responsibly to avoid accumulating high-interest debt.

3. Set Up Accounting and Bookkeeping Systems

Implementing a bookkeeping system early on will help you monitor expenses, revenues, and profits. You can hire an accountant, use accounting software, or even start with a simple spreadsheet if your business is small.

Taking these steps will set a strong foundation for your flooring business, ensuring that you're legally compliant, organized, and prepared for the financial aspects of your operations.

Developing a Comprehensive Business Plan

A well-crafted business plan serves as the roadmap for your flooring business, guiding you through each stage of development and growth. It provides clarity, helps you secure financing if needed, and gives you a clear strategy to follow. In this section, we'll outline the essential elements of a business plan tailored for a flooring business.

Why a Business Plan Matters

A business plan is more than just a document—it's a strategic tool that helps you define your business's goals, understand your target market, and make informed decisions. Here are a few reasons why creating a business plan is beneficial:

1. Clarifies Your Vision and Mission: A business plan helps you clarify your goals and establish the purpose of your company.
2. Guides Growth and Development: As your business grows, a business plan helps keep you on track and focused on achieving specific milestones.
3. Aids in Securing Funding: If you're seeking investors or loans, a well-prepared business plan demonstrates your business's viability.
4. Assists in Risk Management: Identifying potential challenges and developing solutions in advance can help mitigate risks.

Key Components of a Flooring Business Plan

1. Executive Summary
   The executive summary provides a snapshot of your business, highlighting your mission, vision, and goals. While it appears at the beginning of the plan, it's often written last, as it summarizes the details covered in the other sections.

2. Company Description
   This section offers an overview of your company, including its structure (sole proprietorship, LLC, etc.), the services you provide, and your unique selling proposition (USP). Describe what sets your business apart

from others in the flooring industry and what value you bring to your customers.

3. Market Analysis

Market analysis is crucial for understanding the industry landscape, identifying your target audience, and assessing your competition. Include insights into industry trends, customer demographics, and the strengths and weaknesses of competitors in your area.

4. Organization and Management

Describe your business structure, including ownership and key personnel. Outline the roles and responsibilities of each team member, detailing how they contribute to achieving the business's goals. For example, you might explain how installers, sales representatives, and customer service agents each play a role in customer satisfaction and quality control.

5. Product Line or Services

Clearly outline the products and services your flooring business will offer. This may include retail flooring sales, installation, refinishing, or other services. Describe each offering in detail, highlighting what makes it valuable to your target customers. Mention any specialties, such as eco-friendly products or custom installations.

6. Marketing and Sales Strategy

Your marketing plan should detail how you plan to attract and retain customers. Outline your strategies for online and offline marketing, including social media, search engine optimization (SEO), networking with local businesses, and attending trade shows. Define your sales process, including how you'll communicate with clients, conduct consultations, and convert leads into customers.

7. Funding Request (If Applicable)

If you need funding to start or expand your business, include a detailed funding request. Specify how much capital you need, what you'll use it for, and how it will contribute to the growth of your business. Be clear about whether you're seeking loans, investments, or grants.

8. Financial Projections

Financial projections provide insight into the expected revenue, expenses, and profitability of your business. Include a profit and loss statement, cash flow statement, and balance sheet. Project these numbers for at least the first three years, based on realistic assumptions about your sales and growth.

9. Appendix (Optional)

The appendix is a supplementary section where you can include additional documents, such as resumes, product images, or details about your branding. If you've conducted customer surveys or market research, you can also include those findings here.

Tips for Creating a Practical and Effective Business Plan

- Be Realistic: Avoid overly optimistic projections. Use market data and insights from competitor analysis to make grounded assumptions.
- Keep It Clear and Concise: Your business plan doesn't need to be lengthy. Aim to communicate your strategy clearly and efficiently.
- Use Visuals: Charts, graphs, and tables can make financial projections and market data easier to understand.
- Revise Regularly: A business plan isn't static. Revisit and update it as your business evolves to reflect changes in goals, market conditions, and business needs.

A comprehensive business plan will not only guide your daily operations but also provide a strategic foundation for achieving long-term success. With this roadmap in place, you'll be better equipped to navigate the challenges and seize the opportunities that come your way.

Understanding Startup Costs and Funding Options

Starting a flooring business comes with various costs, from equipment and inventory to marketing and administrative expenses. In this section, we'll explore typical startup costs for a flooring business and outline funding options to help cover these initial expenses.

Estimating Startup Costs

To set a realistic budget, break down your expected costs into categories. Knowing your startup costs will also help you determine how much funding you need and when you might expect a return on your investment.

1. Inventory and Supplies

If you're planning to sell flooring materials, inventory costs will be a significant expense. This includes purchasing a variety of flooring types, such as hardwood, laminate, and vinyl. Consider starting with smaller quantities to assess customer preferences and avoid excess stock.

2. Tools and Equipment

Installation-focused businesses will need specialized tools, including saws, drills, tile cutters, adhesives, and safety gear. High-quality tools may come at a premium, but they're essential for efficient, professional work.

3. Vehicles and Transportation

For mobile operations and installations, reliable transportation is crucial. A branded van or truck provides not only transportation but also advertising. Make sure to budget for vehicle maintenance and fuel.

4. Office and Showroom Setup

Whether you're setting up a home office or renting a showroom, create a comfortable, professional space where clients can view samples and consult with you. Costs may include furniture, flooring displays, and office equipment.

5. Marketing and Advertising

Marketing costs are essential for building brand awareness. Consider expenses for website creation, social media marketing, printed materials, and possibly advertising. Allocating a portion of your budget to ongoing marketing will help generate leads.

6. Licensing and Permits
Depending on your location, you may need to pay fees for a business license, contractor license, or permits. These costs vary but are necessary for legal compliance.

7. Insurance
Insurance protects you against potential risks, including liability, property damage, and worker's compensation. Start by obtaining quotes from insurance providers, and make sure you're adequately covered.

8. Operational and Miscellaneous Costs
These might include accounting software, office supplies, and utilities. Planning for these small but essential costs can help you manage your cash flow effectively.

Funding Options for Your Flooring Business

Once you have a clear idea of your startup costs, consider your funding options. Here are some common methods for financing a new business:

1. Personal Savings
Many entrepreneurs use personal savings to fund their startups. This option allows you to maintain full control of your business but can be risky if it depletes your financial resources. Only use savings that you're comfortable allocating to the business.

2. Bank Loans
Banks offer various loan options for small businesses, such as term loans and lines of credit. To qualify, you'll need a solid business plan, good credit history, and possibly collateral. Interest rates vary, so compare different lenders to find favorable terms.

3. Small Business Administration (SBA) Loans
The SBA provides loans specifically for small businesses through partner lenders. These loans often have lower interest rates and more flexible terms. However, the application process can be rigorous, so be prepared with thorough documentation.

4. Investors and Venture Capital

If you're open to sharing ownership, consider seeking funds from investors or venture capitalists. These investors typically look for growth potential and may expect a return on investment. An investor can provide valuable business guidance but may require a portion of your profits or control over certain decisions.

5. Grants and Subsidies

Some organizations offer grants for small businesses, especially if they serve a specific community or meet certain criteria, such as sustainability or veteran-owned businesses. Grants don't need to be repaid, making them an attractive option, though they can be competitive.

6. Crowdfunding

Platforms like Kickstarter, Indiegogo, and GoFundMe allow entrepreneurs to raise funds from the public. Successful crowdfunding campaigns often involve compelling stories and incentives for contributors, such as discounts or early access to products.

7. Family and Friends

Borrowing from family or friends can provide quick, flexible funding, but it's important to formalize the terms to avoid misunderstandings. Clear communication and written agreements are essential for maintaining personal and professional relationships.

Budgeting for Success

Once you secure funding, create a budget that prioritizes essential expenses and minimizes unnecessary spending. A well-planned budget helps you allocate resources efficiently, manage cash flow, and adjust to unexpected costs. Here are some budgeting tips:

- Start Small: Begin with a manageable amount of inventory, marketing, and equipment. As you start earning revenue, reinvest profits to expand.
- Track Every Expense: Use accounting software to monitor expenses in real-time. Regularly review your finances to ensure you're staying on

track.
- Plan for Contingencies: Set aside a small percentage of your budget for unexpected costs, such as equipment repairs or extra marketing efforts.

With a clear understanding of your startup costs and a plan for securing funds, you'll be well-prepared to launch your flooring business on solid financial footing.

Building Your Team and Establishing Roles

As your flooring business grows, having a skilled and reliable team will be essential to delivering high-quality services and satisfying customers. Building a strong team involves not only hiring the right people but also defining their roles clearly and fostering a positive work culture. This section covers strategies for building your team, what roles are critical, and how to develop a cohesive work environment.

Key Roles in a Flooring Business

Depending on the size and focus of your business, your team may include a variety of roles, each contributing to your business's success. Here are some common roles to consider:

1. Flooring Installers
   Flooring installers are at the heart of your business, handling the installation, refinishing, or restoration work. Look for candidates with experience, attention to detail, and knowledge of different materials. Some companies hire contractors or part-time workers to handle overflow projects during busy periods.

2. Sales Representatives
   Sales representatives help generate leads, build client relationships, and convert inquiries into sales. They should be knowledgeable about your products and services, personable, and skilled at closing deals. If you're running a showroom, a dedicated sales team can enhance the

customer experience by offering personalized advice and assistance.

3. Project Managers

A project manager oversees each job from start to finish, ensuring that projects stay on schedule, within budget, and meet quality standards. Project managers coordinate between clients, installers, and suppliers, making sure that every job runs smoothly. They're essential for managing complex projects and maintaining client satisfaction.

4. Customer Service Representatives

Customer service representatives handle inquiries, schedule appointments, and provide after-sales support. This role is crucial for maintaining positive client relationships and managing expectations. Good customer service can lead to repeat business and positive referrals.

5. Administrative Staff

Administrative staff manage the day-to-day operations, including accounting, payroll, inventory management, and purchasing. They ensure that the business operates efficiently behind the scenes, supporting the team in various functions.

Hiring Strategies for Success

Hiring the right people for these roles requires thoughtful planning. Here are some strategies to attract and retain quality team members:

1. Define Clear Job Descriptions

Start by writing detailed job descriptions that outline the responsibilities, required skills, and expectations for each position. This helps attract candidates who are truly qualified and committed to the role.

2. Look for Relevant Experience and Skills

In roles like installation and project management, experience is invaluable. Look for candidates with a proven track record in the flooring or construction industry, along with any relevant certifications or skills.

3. Conduct Thorough Interviews

Interviews are your opportunity to assess a candidate's technical skills, reliability, and fit within your company culture. Ask questions that reveal their problem-solving abilities, work ethic, and approach to customer service.

4. Offer Competitive Compensation and Benefits
Attracting skilled workers often requires offering competitive pay, benefits, and opportunities for growth. If possible, provide perks such as paid time off, health benefits, or professional development to incentivize long-term commitment.

5. Hire on a Trial Basis, If Possible
Hiring on a trial or probationary basis allows you to evaluate a candidate's performance and compatibility with the team before committing to a long-term arrangement. This can be particularly helpful for installer and project manager roles.

Developing a Strong Work Culture

A positive work culture can boost morale, increase productivity, and reduce employee turnover. Here are a few ways to cultivate a supportive and engaging work environment:

1. Set Clear Expectations
From day one, communicate your standards for quality, customer service, and professionalism. Ensure that everyone understands their role and how it contributes to the company's success.

2. Encourage Open Communication
Create an environment where team members feel comfortable sharing ideas, asking questions, and providing feedback. Open communication helps prevent misunderstandings and fosters a sense of camaraderie.

3. Recognize and Reward Hard Work
Acknowledge and reward employees who go above and beyond. Recognition, whether through verbal praise, bonuses, or other incentives, makes employees feel valued and motivates them to continue

performing at their best.

4. Invest in Training and Development

Regular training sessions help your team stay updated on industry trends, new installation techniques, and customer service practices. Investing in their growth shows that you're committed to their success as well as your business's.

5. Promote Teamwork and Respect

Encourage teamwork by promoting collaboration on projects and respecting everyone's contributions. A respectful environment not only improves job satisfaction but also leads to better results for clients.

The Benefits of a Reliable Team

A strong team is more than just a workforce; it's a foundation for your business's reputation, growth, and client satisfaction. Here's why a reliable team matters:

- Consistent Quality: Skilled employees help maintain consistent, high-quality service, leading to positive reviews and referrals.
- Efficient Operations: A well-coordinated team can complete projects on time and within budget, which keeps clients happy and maximizes profitability.
- Customer Loyalty: Positive interactions with knowledgeable and friendly staff create a memorable customer experience that encourages repeat business.

Investing time and resources into building a dependable team is one of the best ways to set your flooring business up for success. With the right people, clear roles, and a positive work culture, you'll be equipped to tackle projects, satisfy clients, and grow your business sustainably.

Creating Efficient Business Processes

Efficiency is key to maximizing profits and maintaining a smooth workflow in any business. In a flooring business, creating efficient processes can help you complete projects on time, reduce costs, and enhance customer satisfaction. In this section, we'll discuss setting up essential business processes that support productivity and improve client experiences.

Process 1: Scheduling and Project Management

Effective scheduling and project management are vital to keeping projects on track. Delays or miscommunication can lead to dissatisfied customers and lost business. Implementing a system that coordinates schedules, tracks project stages, and anticipates potential bottlenecks will help you avoid these issues.

1. Use Project Management Software
   Project management software such as Asana, Trello, or Jobber can help you manage tasks, deadlines, and team assignments. It allows you to break down each project into stages, set deadlines, and assign specific tasks to team members, ensuring accountability.

2. Create Standard Operating Procedures (SOPs)
   Develop SOPs for each stage of the project, from initial consultation to installation and follow-up. SOPs clarify expectations, streamline tasks, and provide a reference for team members, making it easier to maintain consistency and quality across all projects.

3. Plan for Contingencies
   Unexpected challenges are common in flooring projects, from supply delays to inclement weather. Planning for potential delays by building flexibility into your schedule can prevent small setbacks from affecting the entire project timeline.

Process 2: Inventory and Supply Management

Inventory management is essential if you're selling or storing flooring materials. Without an efficient inventory process, you risk overstocking, running out of essential materials, or misplacing products, which can affect project timelines and your bottom line.

1. Implement Inventory Tracking Software

Inventory management tools like QuickBooks, Square, or dedicated flooring software can help you monitor stock levels, order history, and supplier information. This prevents stock shortages and helps you plan orders based on demand.

2. Establish Supplier Relationships

Building strong relationships with suppliers can give you access to better prices, priority ordering, and flexible payment terms. Establish a primary supplier for your main products and maintain a backup supplier for emergencies.

3. Set Up Reorder Points

Calculate minimum stock levels for high-demand materials and set reorder points to avoid shortages. Automated notifications from your inventory software can help you stay on top of orders.

Process 3: Quality Control and Customer Satisfaction

Quality control ensures that every project meets your standards and client expectations. Implementing consistent quality checks throughout each project can reduce mistakes, prevent rework, and improve client satisfaction.

1. Establish a Quality Checklist

Create a checklist that covers each stage of the project, including preparation, installation, and final inspection. Checklists help installers verify that each task meets your standards and provide clients with a sense of thoroughness and professionalism.

2. Conduct a Final Walkthrough

Before handing over the finished project to the client, conduct a final walkthrough with them. This allows you to address any concerns or touch-ups needed and ensures the client is satisfied before signing off on the work.

3. Gather Customer Feedback

Encourage clients to provide feedback on the completed project. Use customer surveys or follow-up calls to gain insights into their experience. Positive feedback can be used in testimonials, while constructive feedback helps you improve.

Process 4: Financial Management and Cash Flow Monitoring

Financial management is crucial for keeping your business profitable. By setting up a system to track expenses, revenues, and cash flow, you'll have a clearer understanding of your financial health and be better prepared for growth.

1. Use Accounting Software

Accounting software such as QuickBooks, Xero, or FreshBooks can help you manage invoices, track expenses, and monitor cash flow. These tools make it easier to generate financial reports, which provide insights into your profitability and areas for improvement.

2. Set Up Invoicing and Payment Policies

Establish clear invoicing terms, such as requiring deposits, progress payments, or final payments upon project completion. Clear payment policies prevent payment delays and provide a steady cash flow to fund operations.

3. Budget for Regular Expenses

Create a monthly budget that includes regular expenses like rent, utilities, inventory, and payroll. Budgeting helps you plan for recurring costs and allocate funds for growth initiatives or unexpected expenses.

Process 5: Marketing and Client Outreach

Marketing is an ongoing process that builds brand awareness, attracts new clients, and nurtures existing relationships. Developing a strategic marketing plan can help your business stay visible and competitive.

1. Use a Content Calendar for Consistent Marketing

A content calendar helps you plan and schedule marketing activities, such as blog posts, social media updates, and email campaigns. Consistency keeps your brand active and engages potential clients.

2. Leverage Customer Reviews and Testimonials

Positive reviews and testimonials are powerful marketing tools. Encourage satisfied clients to leave reviews online, and feature testimonials on your website and social media.

3. Network with Local Businesses

Partnering with real estate agents, interior designers, and home renovation companies can provide a steady stream of client referrals. Networking helps establish your business within the community and expands your customer base.

Benefits of Streamlined Processes

By implementing efficient processes in these areas, you'll benefit from:

- Improved Productivity: Streamlined processes reduce time spent on administrative tasks, freeing up resources for more projects.
- Higher Customer Satisfaction: Clients appreciate businesses that operate smoothly and communicate effectively.
- Cost Savings: Efficient inventory and financial management reduce waste and minimize expenses.
- Scalability: With solid processes in place, your business is better prepared to handle growth and expansion.

Establishing these processes lays the groundwork for a successful and sustainable flooring business, giving you the confidence to tackle challenges and pursue opportunities as they arise.

Chapter 3: Knowing Your Products – Types of Flooring Materials

Overview of Flooring Options

In the flooring business, product knowledge is essential. Each type of flooring material comes with its own benefits, challenges, and ideal applications. By understanding these details, you'll be better equipped to advise clients, make sales, and ensure customer satisfaction. This chapter provides an overview of the main types of flooring materials, including their unique features, pros and cons, and target markets.

The Importance of Product Knowledge

A deep understanding of flooring materials sets your business apart and builds trust with customers. Flooring is a long-term investment, and clients rely on you to recommend solutions that suit their needs, budget, and lifestyle. When you know the ins and outs of each material, you can guide clients through their choices confidently.

Popular Flooring Types

Here is an overview of the most popular types of flooring materials, each with its specific characteristics and ideal applications:

1. Hardwood Flooring

Hardwood is a classic choice known for its timeless beauty and durability. Available in various species like oak, maple, and cherry, hardwood flooring adds value to a property and can last for decades with proper maintenance. It's ideal for residential homes and high-end commercial spaces.

   - Pros: Long lifespan, natural aesthetics, can be refinished multiple times.
   - Cons: Expensive, sensitive to moisture, and requires periodic maintenance.
   - Target Market: Homeowners and businesses looking for premium, elegant flooring solutions.

2. Laminate Flooring

Laminate is an affordable, durable alternative to hardwood, designed to mimic natural wood or stone. It's constructed with a photographic layer on top, which can replicate the appearance of various materials. Laminate is easy to install and is resistant to scratches and wear.

   - Pros: Cost-effective, durable, scratch-resistant, and easy to install.
   - Cons: Not as long-lasting as hardwood, limited refinishing options, can be sensitive to moisture.
   - Target Market: Budget-conscious clients and homeowners seeking a wood-like appearance without the high cost.

3. Vinyl Flooring

Vinyl flooring has come a long way in recent years, with luxury vinyl plank (LVP) and luxury vinyl tile (LVT) providing high-quality, versatile options. It's water-resistant, making it ideal for kitchens, bathrooms, and commercial spaces. Vinyl flooring is also easy to maintain and comes in various styles and colors.

- Pros: Water-resistant, affordable, low maintenance, available in many styles.
   - Cons: Can dent under heavy furniture, may fade with sunlight exposure.
   - Target Market: Residential and commercial clients looking for durable, budget-friendly flooring.

4. Tile Flooring

Tile, including ceramic and porcelain, is a popular choice for areas prone to moisture, such as bathrooms and kitchens. Tile is durable, available in countless designs, and easy to clean. It offers endless customization options, allowing for intricate patterns and unique color combinations.

   - Pros: Water-resistant, durable, easy to clean, customizable.
   - Cons: Hard and cold underfoot, requires grout maintenance, more labor-intensive to install.
   - Target Market: Homeowners and commercial clients needing durable, water-resistant solutions for high-moisture areas.

5. Carpet Flooring

Carpet provides warmth, comfort, and sound insulation, making it a popular choice for bedrooms, living rooms, and offices. It comes in a variety of textures, colors, and materials, from wool to synthetic fibers. Carpeting can be budget-friendly and offers quick installation.

   - Pros: Comfortable, provides sound insulation, quick installation.
   - Cons: Prone to stains, requires regular cleaning, not ideal for high-moisture areas.
   - Target Market: Homeowners, offices, and hospitality clients seeking warmth and comfort.

6. Engineered Wood Flooring

Engineered wood is constructed with a thin layer of hardwood bonded over high-quality plywood, providing the look of hardwood with added stability. It's less prone to expansion and contraction than solid wood, making it suitable for areas where moisture levels fluctuate.

- Pros: Real wood appearance, more stable than solid wood, can be installed in basements.
   - Cons: Limited refinishing options, may be more expensive than laminate.
   - Target Market: Clients who want a hardwood look with enhanced durability and stability.

This overview provides a foundation for understanding each type of flooring. In the following pages, we'll delve into the unique qualities of each material and how to match them with specific client needs.

Hardwood Flooring – Beauty and Longevity

Hardwood flooring is one of the most sought-after choices for its classic look, durability, and timeless appeal. This page dives into the qualities, maintenance needs, and applications of hardwood, helping you understand when to recommend it and how to guide clients in making the right choice.

Types of Hardwood Flooring

Hardwood flooring is available in two main types: solid hardwood and engineered hardwood. Both offer the beauty of real wood, but they differ in construction and durability.

1. Solid Hardwood
   Solid hardwood is made from a single piece of wood and can be sanded and refinished multiple times, making it a long-lasting option. It's best suited for areas with low humidity, as it can expand and contract with changes in moisture levels.

   - Advantages: Exceptional durability, can be refinished, adds value to the property.
   - Limitations: Sensitive to moisture, high installation cost, requires regular maintenance.

2. Engineered Hardwood
Engineered hardwood consists of a top layer of hardwood veneer over plywood or high-density fiberboard. This construction makes it more resistant to moisture and temperature changes, making it suitable for basements and high-humidity areas.

- Advantages: More stable than solid wood, can handle moisture fluctuations, real wood appearance.
- Limitations: Limited refinishing options, may not last as long as solid hardwood.

Popular Wood Species for Flooring

Choosing the right wood species is important, as each type offers different colors, grain patterns, and hardness levels. Here are some popular species:

1. Oak
Oak is one of the most common choices due to its durability, affordability, and classic look. It has a prominent grain pattern and is available in red and white varieties.

2. Maple
Maple has a subtle grain and a lighter color, making it ideal for modern and minimalist designs. It's harder than oak and can withstand heavy traffic, but it can be challenging to stain evenly.

3. Cherry
Cherry wood has a rich, reddish-brown color that deepens over time. Its soft texture makes it more prone to scratches, so it's best suited for low-traffic areas or homes without pets.

4. Walnut
Walnut is prized for its dark, elegant look and smooth grain. It's softer than oak and maple, making it ideal for bedrooms and living rooms rather than high-traffic areas.

5. Hickory

Hickory is known for its distinct grain and color variation. It's one of the hardest domestic woods, making it ideal for high-traffic areas and homes with pets or children.

Benefits of Hardwood Flooring

Hardwood flooring offers numerous benefits, making it a worthwhile investment for many clients:

- Aesthetic Appeal: Hardwood floors have a natural beauty and can enhance the look of any room.
- Long-Term Value: Hardwood can last decades with proper care, and it increases the value of a property.
- Health Benefits: Unlike carpet, hardwood doesn't trap dust, allergens, or pet dander, making it a healthier choice for allergy-prone individuals.
- Eco-Friendly Options: Many hardwood floors come from sustainably managed forests, offering a green option for environmentally conscious clients.

Maintenance and Care

Hardwood flooring is durable but requires regular care to maintain its appearance and extend its lifespan:

1. Regular Cleaning

Sweep or vacuum floors regularly to prevent dirt and grit from scratching the surface. Use a damp mop with a wood-safe cleaner to clean the floor periodically.

2. Avoid Moisture and Humidity

Excessive moisture can warp hardwood, so avoid using wet mops or allowing spills to sit. Use a dehumidifier in humid areas to keep moisture levels stable.

3. Protect Against Scratches

Use area rugs in high-traffic areas, and place felt pads under furniture legs to prevent scratches. Be cautious with high heels and pet claws, as they can scratch the surface.

4. Refinishing

One of the biggest advantages of hardwood is its ability to be sanded and refinished. Refinishing can remove surface scratches and restore the wood's original shine, making the floor look new again.

Ideal Applications and Recommendations

Hardwood flooring is versatile and works well in various settings. However, it's best suited for the following areas:

- Living Rooms and Bedrooms: Hardwood adds warmth and elegance to living spaces and is suitable for low- to moderate-traffic areas.
- Hallways and Dining Rooms: Durable hardwood species like oak or hickory can withstand the wear and tear of high-traffic zones.
- Avoid in Bathrooms and Basements: Due to moisture sensitivity, hardwood isn't ideal for bathrooms or below-grade installations unless using engineered wood designed for these environments.

Hardwood flooring remains a top choice for those seeking elegance, durability, and long-term value. By understanding its benefits, limitations, and care needs, you can confidently recommend it to clients who want a timeless look for their space.

Laminate Flooring – Affordable and Durable

Laminate flooring has gained popularity for its affordability, durability, and versatility. This material offers a stylish, low-maintenance alternative to hardwood and is well-suited for clients looking for a budget-friendly option. Here, we'll explore the benefits, limitations, and applications of laminate flooring and how to guide clients toward this choice.

What is Laminate Flooring?

Laminate flooring is a multi-layered synthetic product designed to imitate the look of natural wood, stone, or tile. It typically consists of four layers:

1. Wear Layer: A clear top layer that protects against scratches, stains, and fading.
2. Decorative Layer: A high-resolution photographic image that mimics wood, tile, or stone.
3. Core Layer: Made of high-density fiberboard (HDF) or medium-density fiberboard (MDF) for stability and impact resistance.
4. Backing Layer: The bottom layer provides moisture resistance and structural support, preventing the floor from warping.

Laminate is often sold in planks that snap together, making installation easy and ideal for DIY projects.

Advantages of Laminate Flooring

Laminate flooring offers several advantages, making it an appealing option for a range of clients:

- Affordable Alternative to Hardwood: Laminate provides a similar look to wood at a fraction of the cost, making it a popular choice for budget-conscious clients.
- Durability and Scratch Resistance: The wear layer on laminate flooring makes it highly resistant to scratches, stains, and fading, even in high-traffic areas.
- Ease of Installation: Laminate is designed for easy, click-lock installation, allowing for faster and more affordable installation compared to other materials.
- Low Maintenance: Laminate requires minimal upkeep, with no need for polishing or waxing. Regular sweeping or vacuuming and occasional mopping are sufficient to maintain its appearance.

Limitations of Laminate Flooring

While laminate has many benefits, it does come with some limitations:

- Moisture Sensitivity: Standard laminate is not waterproof, making it

unsuitable for bathrooms, basements, or areas with high moisture levels.
- Limited Refinishing Options: Unlike hardwood, laminate cannot be sanded or refinished. Once damaged, it typically needs to be replaced.
- Sound and Feel: Some clients may find laminate less authentic in terms of sound and feel compared to real wood, although underlayment can help reduce noise and improve comfort.

Popular Styles of Laminate Flooring

Laminate flooring comes in various styles, allowing clients to achieve different aesthetics. Here are some popular options:

1. Wood-Look Laminate
   Wood-look laminate replicates the appearance of natural wood species, including oak, maple, and walnut. It's available in a range of finishes, from matte to high gloss, providing a close imitation of hardwood floors.

2. Tile and Stone-Look Laminate
   For clients who prefer the look of tile or stone, laminate options mimic ceramic, slate, or marble, offering a sophisticated appearance without the cold, hard feel of actual stone.

3. Textured Laminate
   Textured laminate includes embossing that replicates the grain and texture of real wood, enhancing its visual appeal and making it feel more authentic.

Maintenance and Care

Laminate flooring is easy to maintain, making it a practical choice for busy households. Here's how clients can keep their laminate floors in top condition:

1. Regular Cleaning
   Sweep or vacuum the floor regularly to remove dust and debris. A microfiber mop works well for dry cleaning, as it reduces the risk of scratching.

2. Use a Damp Mop for Deeper Cleaning

For deeper cleaning, use a damp mop with a laminate-safe cleaner. Avoid soaking the floor, as excessive moisture can damage the core layer.

3. Avoid Harsh Cleaners and Polish

Harsh chemicals, abrasive scrubbers, and waxes can damage the wear layer. Always use cleaners designed specifically for laminate floors.

4. Protect from Heavy Furniture and Spills

Use furniture pads to prevent scratches and promptly wipe up spills to avoid moisture damage.

Ideal Applications and Recommendations

Laminate flooring is suitable for a variety of spaces, particularly those where durability and affordability are priorities:

- Living Rooms and Bedrooms: Laminate provides the aesthetic of hardwood, making it a popular choice for living areas and bedrooms.
- Hallways and Entryways: Laminate's durability allows it to withstand the wear of high-traffic areas like hallways.
- Avoid in Bathrooms and Basements: Due to its moisture sensitivity, laminate is not ideal for bathrooms or basements unless using specially designed water-resistant laminate products.

Laminate flooring's combination of affordability, durability, and style versatility makes it a practical choice for clients who want an attractive floor without the higher cost and maintenance requirements of hardwood. By understanding its benefits, limitations, and care needs, you can confidently guide clients toward this cost-effective solution for their spaces.

Vinyl Flooring – Versatility and Durability

Vinyl flooring has evolved significantly, with luxury vinyl plank (LVP) and luxury vinyl tile (LVT) now offering realistic wood and stone looks at a fraction of the cost. Known for its water resistance, durability, and style versatility, vinyl is a great choice for clients looking for low-maintenance, budget-friendly options. This section covers the characteristics, advantages, and applications of vinyl flooring.

What is Vinyl Flooring?

Vinyl flooring is a synthetic material made from polyvinyl chloride (PVC) and is available in several forms, including sheets, planks, and tiles. It's known for its durability, water resistance, and ease of installation. The main types of vinyl flooring are:

1. Luxury Vinyl Plank (LVP)
   LVP is designed to resemble hardwood and is available in various colors and grain patterns. Its plank structure gives it a realistic wood appearance, and it can be installed as a floating floor, making it a popular choice for DIY installations.

2. Luxury Vinyl Tile (LVT)
   LVT mimics the look of stone or ceramic tile and is available in various shapes and sizes. It provides a sophisticated appearance and can be installed with or without grout to achieve a tile look.

3. Sheet Vinyl
   Sheet vinyl is sold in large, continuous rolls and is ideal for covering large areas with minimal seams. It's often more budget-friendly than LVP or LVT and is highly water-resistant, making it a practical choice for bathrooms and kitchens.

Advantages of Vinyl Flooring

Vinyl flooring offers a range of benefits, making it suitable for a variety of clients and settings:

- Water Resistance: Vinyl is highly water-resistant, with some types even being waterproof. This makes it ideal for moisture-prone areas like kitchens, bathrooms, and basements.

- Durability: Vinyl is resistant to scratches, stains, and dents, even in high-traffic areas. Its wear layer adds to its durability and protects against daily wear and tear.
- Comfort and Sound Absorption: Vinyl flooring provides a softer feel underfoot compared to tile or hardwood, and it reduces noise, making it a good choice for multi-story homes or apartments.
- Easy Maintenance: Vinyl is low-maintenance and doesn't require sealing or refinishing. Regular sweeping and mopping are sufficient to keep it looking good.
- Affordability: Compared to hardwood or stone, vinyl is budget-friendly, offering a high-end look without the high-end cost.

Limitations of Vinyl Flooring

While vinyl has many advantages, there are a few considerations to keep in mind:

- Susceptible to Fading: Prolonged exposure to direct sunlight can cause vinyl to fade, so it may not be ideal for areas with intense sunlight unless UV-protected.
- Potential for Indentations: Heavy furniture or sharp objects can leave indentations on vinyl flooring, particularly on softer varieties.
- Environmental Impact: Vinyl is made from synthetic materials, and while there are some eco-friendly options, it's not as environmentally sustainable as natural materials like wood or stone.

Popular Styles of Vinyl Flooring

Vinyl flooring is available in a variety of styles to suit different tastes and interiors:

1. Wood-Look Vinyl
   Wood-look vinyl mimics the appearance of hardwood, with options available in various colors, grain patterns, and textures. It's ideal for clients who want the look of wood without the maintenance.

2. Stone-Look Vinyl
   Stone-look vinyl replicates the appearance of natural stone such as

slate, marble, or granite. It's popular for bathrooms, kitchens, and entryways where a durable, water-resistant surface is needed.

3. Patterned Vinyl

For a more unique look, patterned vinyl offers designs such as geometric shapes, florals, and abstract patterns. This style is ideal for clients seeking a distinctive floor that makes a statement.

Maintenance and Care

Vinyl flooring is known for its low-maintenance requirements, making it a practical choice for busy households:

1. Routine Cleaning

Sweep or vacuum regularly to remove dust and debris. Mopping with a vinyl-safe cleaner will keep the floor looking fresh without damaging the surface.

2. Avoid Abrasive Cleaners and Tools

Avoid using abrasive scrubbers or harsh chemicals, as these can damage the wear layer and reduce the floor's longevity.

3. Protect from Heavy Items and Sharp Objects

Use furniture pads to prevent indentations, and be cautious with sharp objects to avoid punctures or scratches.

Ideal Applications and Recommendations

Vinyl flooring is extremely versatile and can be installed in almost any room of the house:

- Kitchens and Bathrooms: Vinyl's water resistance makes it ideal for kitchens and bathrooms, where moisture is a concern.
- Basements: LVP and LVT are suitable for basements, as they can handle humidity and occasional moisture better than hardwood.
- Living Rooms and Bedrooms: With its variety of designs and comfort underfoot, vinyl is also a good choice for living spaces and bedrooms.

Vinyl flooring's combination of water resistance, durability, and aesthetic variety makes it a versatile and practical choice for many applications. With options ranging from realistic wood and stone to bold patterns, vinyl can meet a variety of style preferences and functional needs.

Tile Flooring – Durability and Design Flexibility

Tile flooring is a popular choice for spaces that require water resistance and durability. Known for its versatility in design, tile offers a wide range of colors, patterns, and finishes, making it suitable for various settings, from bathrooms to commercial spaces. This section will cover the types, advantages, and care requirements of tile flooring.

Types of Tile Flooring

There are several types of tile flooring, each with unique properties and suitable applications. The most common include:

1. Ceramic Tile
   Made from natural clay, ceramic tile is fired at high temperatures to create a durable, water-resistant surface. It's available in a range of colors, textures, and finishes, making it a versatile option.

   - Advantages: Affordable, water-resistant, easy to clean.
   - Limitations: Less durable than porcelain, may chip or crack under heavy impact.

2. Porcelain Tile
   Porcelain is a type of ceramic tile fired at even higher temperatures, resulting in a denser, more durable material. It's more resistant to water and stains than standard ceramic, making it ideal for high-traffic and moisture-prone areas.

   - Advantages: Highly durable, low water absorption, can withstand heavy wear.

- Limitations: More expensive than ceramic, harder to cut, may require professional installation.

3. Stone Tile
   Stone tiles, such as marble, granite, and slate, offer a natural, luxurious appearance and are often used in high-end applications. Stone is available in various finishes, including polished, honed, and tumbled.

   - Advantages: Unique, natural look; very durable.
   - Limitations: Requires sealing, can be slippery when polished, often more expensive.

4. Glass Tile
   Glass tiles are often used as accents or in smaller areas, like backsplashes or shower walls. They're highly resistant to stains and moisture but can be more delicate than other tile types.

   - Advantages: Stain-resistant, reflective qualities enhance light.
   - Limitations: Prone to chipping, slippery when wet, limited use in flooring.

Advantages of Tile Flooring

Tile offers several benefits that make it a practical choice for many spaces:

- Water Resistance: Most types of tile are water-resistant, making them ideal for kitchens, bathrooms, and other moisture-prone areas.
- Durability: Tile is highly durable and can withstand heavy traffic, making it suitable for both residential and commercial spaces.
- Design Flexibility: Tile is available in a variety of sizes, colors, and patterns, allowing for endless customization options.
- Low Maintenance: Tile is easy to clean and maintain, requiring only regular sweeping and mopping to keep it looking new.

Limitations of Tile Flooring

Despite its advantages, tile flooring has some limitations:

- Cold and Hard Underfoot: Tile can feel cold and hard, which may not be ideal for living spaces where comfort is a priority.
- Requires Grout Maintenance: Grout lines need regular cleaning and occasional resealing to prevent stains and discoloration.
- Installation Complexity: Tile installation requires precision and often professional skills, especially with porcelain or stone tiles.

Popular Styles of Tile Flooring

Tile flooring offers various design options to suit different aesthetics:

1. Wood-Look Tile

Wood-look tile mimics the appearance of hardwood, offering the beauty of wood with the water resistance of tile. It's perfect for bathrooms, kitchens, and basements.

2. Patterned and Mosaic Tiles

Patterned tiles add character to floors and walls, with options for geometric, floral, and abstract designs. Mosaic tiles, often used as accents, add visual interest and can be used to create custom designs.

3. Natural Stone Appearance

Stone-look tiles replicate the texture and color of natural stone without the higher cost and maintenance. They are ideal for creating an upscale, natural look in any space.

Maintenance and Care

Tile flooring is relatively low-maintenance, but proper care can prolong its appearance and durability:

1. Regular Cleaning

Sweep or vacuum regularly to remove dirt and debris. Use a damp mop with a tile-safe cleaner to keep the surface clean.

2. Grout Maintenance

Grout can become stained over time, so regular scrubbing with a grout cleaner is essential. Sealing grout every few years helps protect it from stains and moisture.

3. Preventing Scratches and Cracks
While tile is durable, sharp or heavy objects can cause damage. Use area rugs in high-traffic areas, and be cautious with heavy furniture or appliances.

Ideal Applications and Recommendations

Tile flooring is versatile and suitable for various areas, especially those exposed to moisture:

- Bathrooms and Kitchens: Tile's water resistance and easy maintenance make it ideal for wet areas.
- Entryways and Hallways: Durable and resistant to dirt, tile is suitable for entryways and high-traffic areas.
- Commercial Spaces: Tile is commonly used in commercial settings due to its durability and low maintenance needs.

Tile flooring's combination of durability, design options, and water resistance makes it a versatile choice for both residential and commercial applications. By understanding the types, benefits, and care requirements of tile, you can confidently guide clients in selecting the best tile for their needs.

Chapter 4: Marketing Your Flooring Business for Growth

Understanding Your Target Market

Effective marketing starts with understanding your target market—the customers you aim to attract. Knowing who your ideal clients are, what they value, and where they spend time can help you tailor your marketing efforts to resonate with them. In this chapter, we'll cover the essentials of marketing for a flooring business, beginning with identifying your target market.

Why Defining Your Target Market is Important

Your target market encompasses the people most likely to need and want your services. By defining this group clearly, you can create messages that appeal directly to their needs, saving time and money by focusing on the most relevant audience. A well-defined target market enables you to:

1. Customize Marketing Messages: Craft messages that resonate with specific customer needs, increasing the chances of attracting interest.
2. Focus on Effective Channels: Know where your audience spends time and focus your marketing efforts on those platforms.
3. Build Stronger Connections: By speaking to their needs and concerns, you're more likely to build trust and long-term relationships.

Identifying Your Ideal Customer

To define your target market, think about the specific types of clients who would benefit most from your services. Here are key characteristics to consider:

1. Demographics
   Demographics help you understand the basic attributes of your potential customers. Key demographic factors for a flooring business might include:

   - Age: Are they young families, retirees, or professionals?
   - Income Level: Does your service appeal more to high-income clients or those on a budget?
   - Homeownership: Are your clients mostly homeowners, property managers, or business owners?

2. Geographic Location
   For local businesses, targeting customers within a specific geographic range is essential. Consider the neighborhoods, cities, or regions where your potential clients live and focus your marketing there. Highlight your familiarity with local trends, building codes, and customer preferences.

3. Psychographics

Psychographics refer to your customers' values, lifestyle, and purchasing habits. Think about what motivates them to purchase flooring:

- Quality vs. Budget: Do they prioritize high-quality, long-lasting floors, or are they looking for affordable options?
- Eco-Consciousness: Are they interested in sustainable, eco-friendly flooring materials?
- Aesthetic Preferences: Are they drawn to modern, rustic, or traditional styles?

4. Behavioral Traits

Observing customer behavior can give insights into how they make decisions. For example:

- Buying Frequency: Are they likely to replace their floors frequently, such as landlords, or invest in one-time, high-quality installations?
- Decision-Making Process: Do they rely heavily on reviews, personal recommendations, or consultations?

Conducting Market Research

To understand your target market, it's essential to conduct market research. Here are some ways to gather information:

1. Online Surveys and Polls

Use online survey tools like Google Forms or SurveyMonkey to ask existing clients about their preferences, budget, and priorities. This feedback provides valuable insights into customer needs.

2. Social Media Insights

If you have a social media presence, use analytics tools to view data on your followers' demographics and engagement patterns. This information can help you refine your content to better appeal to your audience.

3. Competitor Analysis

Study competitors to see who they're targeting and how they're positioning their brand. Look at their social media, website, and customer reviews to understand their approach and identify any gaps you could fill.

4. Customer Feedback and Testimonials

Gather feedback from your past clients to identify common themes in satisfaction and pain points. Positive reviews and testimonials can reveal what clients value most, while constructive feedback highlights areas for improvement.

Creating Customer Personas

A customer persona is a detailed profile of your ideal customer. Based on the data you've gathered, create a few personas representing different segments of your market. Here's an example:

- Persona Name: Susan the Homeowner
- Demographics: 45-year-old homeowner, married with two children, upper-middle income
- Psychographics: Values quality and sustainability, prefers natural materials, and is eco-conscious
- Buying Behavior: Likely to choose flooring that's safe, eco-friendly, and matches a modern aesthetic; often reads reviews before purchasing

By creating personas like this, you'll be able to craft marketing messages that speak directly to the motivations and values of each customer segment.

Key Takeaways for Defining Your Target Market

Understanding your target market is the foundation for successful marketing. By defining your ideal customer, you can focus your resources on reaching the people most likely to hire you. As we move through this chapter, you'll see how to apply this understanding to choose the best marketing channels and craft messages that capture attention.

Developing Your Brand Identity

Your brand identity is the foundation of your marketing efforts. It's what sets your business apart from competitors and creates a lasting impression on clients. A strong brand identity includes your business's visuals, tone, and values, and helps you connect emotionally with customers. In this section, we'll explore how to establish a brand that resonates with your target market.

Key Elements of Brand Identity

Creating a cohesive brand identity involves several key elements:

1. Brand Name and Logo
   Your brand name should be easy to remember and relevant to your services. A unique, professional logo serves as the visual anchor of your brand, appearing on everything from business cards to trucks. Consistency in your logo's appearance and placement helps reinforce your brand.

2. Color Scheme and Design Style
   Choose colors and a design style that reflect your brand's personality. For instance, earthy tones may appeal to environmentally conscious clients, while bold colors can convey energy and creativity. Ensure that your colors and fonts are consistent across all materials, from your website to printed brochures.

3. Tagline or Slogan
   A catchy tagline communicates your unique selling proposition (USP) in just a few words. It should quickly convey what sets you apart, such as, "Quality Floors, Reliable Service" or "Transforming Spaces, One Floor at a Time."

4. Brand Voice and Messaging
   Your brand voice is the tone and style in which you communicate with clients. Are you formal and professional, friendly and approachable, or perhaps a mix of both? Your voice should align with your target

audience. For example, if your target market is young families, a warm and conversational tone may resonate more.

Crafting Your Brand Story

A brand story explains the motivation and values behind your business, helping potential clients connect with you on a personal level. Think of your brand story as the "why" behind your business.

Here's an example:
"After years of working in the flooring industry, I saw an opportunity to create a business that prioritized craftsmanship and customer satisfaction. Our company's mission is to provide clients with high-quality flooring that lasts and enhances their living spaces. We believe that every floor should tell a story and contribute to a home's beauty and comfort."

A compelling brand story makes your business more relatable and memorable. When clients understand the passion behind your business, they're more likely to trust and choose you.

Connecting Your Brand with Your USP

Your unique selling proposition (USP) is the aspect that makes your business stand out. Integrating your USP into your brand identity reinforces what makes you different and valuable. Here are a few ways to tie your USP into your branding:

- Emphasize Quality: If quality is your focus, use words like "excellence," "craftsmanship," and "attention to detail" in your messaging. Your materials should also reflect this, with high-quality photos and polished designs.
- Highlight Sustainability: For an eco-friendly brand, use green tones, nature-inspired designs, and messaging that emphasizes sustainability, such as "Eco-conscious flooring for a better tomorrow."
- Speed and Reliability: If fast service is your USP, a tagline like "Floors Installed in a Flash" or "Timely and Trustworthy" reinforces your

commitment to efficiency.

Building Brand Trust through Consistency

Consistency is essential to brand recognition and trust. When clients see the same brand colors, tone, and style across all platforms, they're more likely to remember and trust your business. Here's how to maintain brand consistency:

1. Website and Social Media
   Your website and social media should reflect your brand's identity through visuals and tone. Use the same colors, logo, and language to create a cohesive experience across platforms.

2. Print Materials and Signage
   Ensure that brochures, business cards, and signs align with your brand. These materials are often a client's first impression, so they should be polished and consistent with your digital presence.

3. Customer Experience
   From phone calls to consultations, every client interaction should reflect your brand's values and voice. Train your team to communicate in a way that reinforces your brand and delivers a consistent experience.

Tips for Strengthening Your Brand Over Time

Building a brand is an ongoing process that evolves as your business grows. Here are some strategies to keep your brand strong:

- Listen to Customer Feedback: Regularly seek feedback from clients to understand how they perceive your brand and identify areas for improvement.
- Keep Up with Industry Trends: Stay updated on design and service trends in the flooring industry to ensure your brand remains relevant and appealing.
- Invest in Professional Design: If your brand materials look outdated, consider refreshing your logo, website, or other visuals to maintain a modern appearance.

A well-defined brand identity helps you stand out, attract the right customers, and foster loyalty. By focusing on what makes your business unique and maintaining consistency across all touchpoints, you can create a memorable brand that clients trust and recommend.

Building an Effective Online Presence

An online presence is essential for any business today, as it helps clients find and learn about your services before making a decision. This section covers how to create a professional website, leverage social media, and use online directories to reach potential clients effectively.

Creating a Professional Website

Your website is often the first impression clients have of your business. A well-designed, informative website can boost credibility and make it easy for clients to engage with your services.

1. Homepage and Contact Information
   The homepage should clearly convey who you are, what you offer, and why clients should choose you. Include a prominent call-to-action (CTA) like "Get a Free Estimate" or "Contact Us Today." Contact information should be easy to find, with phone numbers, email addresses, and links to social media.

2. About Us and Services Pages
   The "About Us" page gives clients insight into your background, values, and unique approach. Include your brand story and emphasize any certifications, experience, or specializations. On the "Services" page, provide details about the types of flooring you offer, installation services, and any additional options like refinishing or repair.

3. Gallery or Portfolio
   Showcase high-quality images of your completed projects to give

potential clients a visual idea of your work quality and style range. Use before-and-after photos, if possible, as they help clients envision the transformation you can bring.

4. Customer Testimonials and Reviews

Adding testimonials builds credibility by showing positive feedback from satisfied clients. Encourage clients to leave reviews, and showcase these on your website to increase trust and engagement.

5. Blog for SEO and Client Engagement

A blog with useful articles about flooring trends, maintenance tips, or renovation advice can boost your search engine optimization (SEO) and attract potential clients. It also demonstrates your expertise and commitment to helping clients make informed decisions.

Utilizing Social Media for Brand Awareness

Social media platforms allow you to engage directly with clients, showcase your work, and build brand awareness. Choose platforms that align with your audience, such as:

1. Instagram and Pinterest

Visual platforms like Instagram and Pinterest are ideal for sharing images of your work, inspiration boards, and design ideas. Use hashtags related to flooring, renovations, and interior design to increase visibility.

2. Facebook

Facebook allows you to connect with local communities, run ads, and share updates. Consider joining local groups where homeowners or property managers may seek flooring recommendations or advice.

3. LinkedIn

For networking and connecting with other professionals in real estate, construction, and interior design, LinkedIn can be valuable. Share content about industry trends, new services, or completed projects to build credibility and connections.

4. Engagement and Posting Strategy

Posting consistently is key to maintaining an active presence. Create a posting schedule and use a mix of content types, like project highlights, client testimonials, tips, and industry insights. Respond promptly to comments and messages to demonstrate responsiveness and customer care.

Listing Your Business on Online Directories

Online directories help clients discover local businesses. Registering your business on directories and review sites improves your online visibility and credibility. Key directories include:

1. Google My Business (GMB)

Google My Business is crucial for local SEO and appearing in local searches. Setting up a GMB profile allows you to show your business location, hours, contact information, and reviews on Google's search results and Maps. Regularly update your profile and encourage satisfied clients to leave reviews.

2. Yelp and Angie's List

Platforms like Yelp and Angie's List are popular for home services, and many clients rely on reviews to make decisions. Ensure your information is accurate and complete, and respond to reviews, both positive and negative, to show your commitment to customer service.

3. Houzz

Houzz is a specialized platform for home improvement and interior design, making it a great choice for flooring businesses. Set up a profile showcasing your projects, services, and client reviews to attract potential customers interested in home renovations.

4. Local Business Directories

Listing your business on local directories, such as the Chamber of Commerce website or local home service directories, can further increase your visibility in your community.

Tips for Managing Your Online Presence

Managing your online presence doesn't have to be overwhelming. Here are some strategies for success:

- Use a Content Calendar: Plan your social media and blog content in advance to ensure consistency and reduce last-minute stress.
- Monitor Analytics: Review website and social media analytics to see what content resonates with your audience. Adjust your strategy based on these insights.
- Respond Promptly: Quick responses to inquiries and reviews show professionalism and dedication to customer satisfaction.

Building an online presence is a gradual process, with consistent effort, it can significantly enhance your brand visibility, attract more clients, and establish your business as a trusted provider in your community.

Leveraging Content Marketing and SEO

Content marketing and search engine optimization (SEO) are essential strategies for attracting clients to your flooring business through online searches. By providing valuable content and optimizing it for search engines, you can drive traffic to your website, build credibility, and turn visitors into clients. This section covers content marketing basics and tips for optimizing your online presence.

Creating Valuable Content

Content marketing involves creating and sharing content that informs, educates, or inspires your audience. For a flooring business, content can range from blog posts and videos to how-to guides and project galleries. Here's how to get started with content marketing:

1. Identify Topics Relevant to Your Audience
   Choose topics that address your audience's needs, questions, and interests. Examples might include "Choosing the Right Flooring for Your Home," "How to Care for Hardwood Floors," or "Top Flooring Trends for 2024."

2. Create Different Types of Content
Different types of content can engage various audience segments. Consider creating:

- Blog Posts: Written articles that answer common questions, provide tips, or highlight industry trends.
- Videos: Video content, such as installation demos, product comparisons, or client testimonials, can be highly engaging.
- Infographics: Visual guides or infographics are effective for summarizing information, such as flooring maintenance steps or design trends.
- Case Studies: Showcase successful projects to give clients insight into your process, skills, and results.

3. Engage Your Audience
Content that encourages engagement, such as comments or shares, is more likely to reach a wider audience. Encourage clients to share your content, leave comments, or ask questions to build a sense of community around your brand.

Optimizing for SEO

SEO involves optimizing your website and content to rank higher in search engine results. By appearing at the top of search results, you increase the chances of attracting new clients. Here are key SEO strategies:

1. Keyword Research
Identify keywords and phrases that potential clients might search for, such as "flooring installation," "best hardwood floors," or "eco-friendly flooring." Tools like Google Keyword Planner, Ahrefs, or Ubersuggest can help you find relevant keywords with high search volume.

2. On-Page SEO

Optimize individual pages on your website for specific keywords. Here's how:

- Title Tags: Include your primary keyword in the page title to tell search engines what the page is about.
- Headings and Subheadings: Use keywords in headings (H1, H2, H3 tags) to structure content and improve readability.
- Meta Descriptions: Write concise, descriptive meta descriptions with keywords to encourage clicks from search engine results.
- Image Alt Text: Add keywords to image alt text to improve image search ranking and accessibility.

3. Quality Content and Length

High-quality, in-depth content ranks better than short, surface-level content. Aim to write articles that are at least 1,000 words long, covering topics thoroughly to satisfy both readers and search engines.

4. Internal and External Links

Use internal links to connect related pages on your website, helping visitors navigate and encouraging them to stay longer. External links to authoritative sources can add credibility to your content and improve SEO.

5. Mobile-Friendly Design

Google prioritizes mobile-friendly websites in search results. Ensure your website is optimized for mobile devices by using responsive design, which adjusts content layout based on screen size.

Content Distribution and Promotion

Creating great content is only the first step. To reach a broader audience, distribute and promote your content across multiple channels:

1. Social Media Platforms

Share blog posts, videos, and infographics on your social media channels. Use relevant hashtags and tag local businesses or influencers to increase reach.

2. Email Marketing

Send regular newsletters with links to new blog posts or videos, industry updates, and exclusive offers. Email marketing keeps your brand top of mind and encourages repeat visits to your website.

3. Collaborate with Local Influencers

Partnering with local influencers, such as interior designers or home renovation bloggers, can help you reach new audiences. Offer them insights, samples, or even co-host online events to showcase your expertise.

4. Use Paid Ads for Wider Reach

Consider using paid ads, such as Google Ads or Facebook Ads, to reach a larger audience. These ads can be targeted based on location, interests, and demographics, increasing your chances of connecting with potential clients.

Tracking and Analyzing Results

To improve your content marketing and SEO efforts, track performance and analyze the results:

1. Google Analytics

Google Analytics provides insights into website traffic, user behavior, and engagement. Review which pages receive the most traffic, how long visitors stay, and which keywords drive the most visits.

2. SEO Tools

SEO tools like Ahrefs, SEMrush, or Moz can track keyword rankings, backlink profiles, and site performance. Regularly reviewing these metrics allows you to adjust your strategy based on what works best.

3. Social Media Analytics

Most social media platforms offer analytics tools to help you measure engagement, reach, and follower growth. Use these insights to refine your content and posting strategy.

By creating valuable content and optimizing it for search engines, you can attract more clients and establish your business as a trusted source in the flooring industry. With consistent effort and tracking, content marketing and SEO can be powerful tools to grow your online presence and drive business growth.

Running Targeted Advertising Campaigns

Targeted advertising can help you reach potential clients who are actively looking for flooring services or who may need them soon. By selecting the right platforms and creating compelling ads, you can increase visibility and attract new clients. This section explores different types of advertising channels and provides tips for running successful ad campaigns.

Choosing the Right Advertising Channels

Not all advertising channels are equal, and selecting the right ones depends on where your target market spends time. Here are some popular advertising channels for flooring businesses:

1. Google Ads
   Google Ads allows you to reach clients searching for flooring services by displaying your ads at the top of search results. Use keyword-based targeting to capture high-intent searches, such as "flooring installer near me" or "hardwood flooring installation."

2. Facebook and Instagram Ads
   Facebook and Instagram are ideal for visual advertising, allowing you to showcase before-and-after photos, videos, or client testimonials. With detailed targeting options, you can reach users based on location, interests, demographics, and behaviors, ensuring your ads reach relevant audiences.

3. YouTube Ads
   YouTube allows you to advertise using video ads before, during, or after other videos. Video ads can showcase your expertise, demonstrate

installation techniques, or offer maintenance tips, which can increase credibility and interest in your services.

4. Local Newspaper and Magazine Ads

If your target audience includes local homeowners or property managers, consider advertising in local newspapers or home improvement magazines. These ads help establish your business in the community and are great for clients who prefer traditional media.

5. Direct Mail

Direct mail campaigns allow you to reach potential clients in a specific geographic area. Brochures, postcards, or flyers highlighting your services, special offers, or seasonal promotions can generate leads, especially if you target neighborhoods with older homes or areas with high remodeling activity.

Creating Effective Ad Content

Compelling ad content is essential to capture attention and drive action. Here are some tips for creating ads that resonate with your audience:

1. Focus on Benefits

Highlight the benefits your services offer rather than just listing features. Instead of saying, "We install hardwood floors," emphasize benefits like "Transform your home with beautiful, durable hardwood floors that increase property value."

2. Use High-Quality Images and Videos

Visual appeal is important, especially on social media. Use professional-quality images or videos that showcase your work. Before-and-after shots or videos of your team in action can be very effective.

3. Include a Clear Call to Action (CTA)

Every ad should include a CTA that tells clients what to do next, such as "Get a Free Quote," "Schedule a Consultation," or "Call Today for Special Discounts." A strong CTA encourages clients to take the next step.

4. Offer Limited-Time Promotions

Limited-time offers can create urgency and motivate potential clients to act. Consider offering a discount on installation, free consultations, or seasonal promotions.

Setting Your Advertising Budget

Setting a budget helps you manage costs and measure the effectiveness of your campaigns. Here's how to establish a budget for your ads:

1. Determine Your Monthly Spend

Start by estimating how much you're willing to spend on advertising monthly. For online ads, platforms like Google Ads and Facebook allow you to set a daily or monthly budget and adjust as needed.

2. Allocate to Different Channels

Divide your budget among various channels based on which ones are most effective for your audience. For example, if your audience is active on social media, allocate more of your budget to Facebook and Instagram ads.

3. Test and Adjust

Start with a smaller budget to test which ads perform best. Track metrics like click-through rates, conversions, and return on ad spend (ROAS). Adjust your budget allocation based on which platforms and ad types are generating the best results.

Tracking and Measuring Ad Performance

Measuring the performance of your ads allows you to understand what's working and refine your approach. Key performance indicators (KPIs) include:

1. Click-Through Rate (CTR)

The CTR indicates the percentage of people who clicked on your ad after seeing it. A high CTR suggests your ad is engaging and relevant to your audience.

2. Conversion Rate

Conversion rate measures the percentage of people who completed a desired action, such as filling out a contact form or scheduling a consultation. It's a critical metric for evaluating ad effectiveness.

3. Cost Per Click (CPC)

CPC is the amount you pay each time someone clicks on your ad. Monitoring CPC helps ensure you're not overpaying for clicks and can help you adjust bids if needed.

4. Return on Ad Spend (ROAS)

ROAS measures the revenue generated for every dollar spent on advertising. A positive ROAS indicates a profitable campaign, while a low ROAS may suggest you need to refine your targeting, ad content, or budget.

5. A/B Testing

A/B testing, or split testing, involves running two versions of an ad to see which performs better. Experiment with different images, headlines, or CTAs to optimize your ads for maximum impact.

Ad Campaign Optimization Tips

Once you've run initial campaigns, optimize them for better results:

- Refine Targeting: Review audience insights to understand who is responding to your ads and adjust targeting based on demographics, interests, or location.
- Update Creative Regularly: Ads can become stale over time. Refresh visuals and messaging periodically to maintain audience engagement.
- Reinvest in High-Performing Ads: Allocate more budget to the ads and platforms generating the highest returns to maximize effectiveness.

Running targeted ad campaigns can enhance visibility, generate leads, and drive growth for your flooring business. With the right platforms, compelling content, and performance tracking, advertising can become a powerful tool in your marketing strategy.

Chapter 5: Building Customer Relationships for Long-Term Success

The Importance of Customer Relationships in Business Growth

In the flooring business, customer relationships are key to long-term success. Satisfied clients are more likely to refer you to others, leave positive reviews, and return for future projects. Building strong relationships with clients not only supports steady business growth but also strengthens your reputation in the community. This chapter explores how to create, nurture, and maintain meaningful customer relationships.

Benefits of Strong Customer Relationships

Investing in customer relationships provides several benefits that directly impact your business growth:

1. Increased Referrals
   Happy customers are likely to recommend your services to friends, family, and neighbors, leading to valuable referrals. Referrals are often high-quality leads because they come from trusted recommendations.

2. Higher Customer Retention
   Clients who feel valued and appreciated are more likely to return for future projects. Building strong relationships reduces the likelihood of clients seeking services from competitors.

3. Positive Online Reviews
   Satisfied clients are more inclined to leave positive reviews, which enhance your credibility and attract new clients. Consistently positive feedback on platforms like Google, Yelp, and Houzz strengthens your online presence and reputation.

4. Loyalty and Brand Ambassadorship
   Long-term customers can become brand ambassadors, advocating for your business within their networks and endorsing your services to others. This organic promotion can be invaluable for your reputation.

Establishing Trust from the Start

Building trust begins with the first interaction you have with a potential client. Here are some steps to establish a solid foundation of trust:

1. Clear Communication
   From the initial consultation, be transparent about your services, costs, and timeline. Clear, honest communication demonstrates your professionalism and commitment to meeting client expectations.

2. Follow Through on Promises
   Reliability is essential for building trust. Always follow through on what you promise, whether it's providing an estimate, showing up for an

appointment, or meeting project deadlines.

3. Listen to Client Needs

Take the time to understand each client's specific needs, preferences, and concerns. Personalized service shows clients that you're attentive and genuinely interested in helping them achieve their vision.

4. Provide Honest Recommendations

Offer professional recommendations that suit the client's needs, even if it means suggesting a less expensive or different flooring option. Clients appreciate honesty, and this builds credibility.

Personalized service sets you apart from competitors and makes clients feel valued. Small gestures can make a big difference in the client's experience with your business.

1. Remember Client Preferences

Take note of client preferences, such as specific design styles, color schemes, or project requirements. Mentioning these details during follow-up conversations shows that you're attentive and considerate.

2. Send Thank You Notes

A handwritten thank-you note or follow-up email after project completion leaves a lasting impression. Thank clients for choosing your business, acknowledge their trust in your services, and encourage them to reach out with any questions or concerns.

3. Celebrate Milestones

If clients are completing a significant home renovation or celebrating a special occasion, acknowledge it. Sending a small gift or card can enhance your relationship with the client and encourage future interactions.

4. Offer Maintenance Tips and Advice

Providing clients with tips on how to care for their new floors shows that you care about their long-term satisfaction. It also reinforces your expertise and positions you as a trusted resource.

Effective Communication Throughout the Project

Consistent communication is essential throughout a flooring project. Keeping clients updated and addressing concerns promptly helps prevent misunderstandings and demonstrates your commitment to quality.

1. Set Clear Expectations
   Before beginning the project, discuss the timeline, scope, and any potential challenges. Addressing expectations upfront minimizes the risk of surprises and helps the project run smoothly.

2. Provide Regular Updates
   Update clients on the project's progress, especially if there are delays or changes. This level of transparency reassures clients that you're attentive to the project and committed to keeping them informed.

3. Address Concerns Promptly
   If a client raises a concern, address it promptly. Quick responses show respect for their time and demonstrate your dedication to client satisfaction.

4. Request Feedback at Project Completion
   After completing the project, ask clients for feedback. Whether through an email, a survey, or a brief conversation, feedback allows you to understand what went well and identify areas for improvement.

Building customer relationships is about more than just completing a project; it's about creating an experience that leaves clients feeling valued and appreciated. When you prioritize relationships, clients are more likely to become loyal supporters, refer others, and return for future projects. By consistently delivering on promises, providing personalized service, and maintaining open communication, you can establish a strong foundation for long-term success in your flooring business.

Providing Exceptional Customer Service

Exceptional customer service is a key component in building lasting relationships with clients. When clients feel valued and supported, they're more likely to trust your business, recommend you to others, and return for future projects. This section explores the elements of outstanding customer service and how to implement them in your flooring business.

Understanding the Elements of Great Customer Service

Customer service goes beyond answering questions; it's about creating a positive experience at every stage of the client's journey. Here are some essential elements of exceptional service:

1. Responsiveness
   Responding promptly to inquiries, whether through phone, email, or social media, shows that you respect clients' time and are eager to assist. A quick response can set the tone for a positive experience, even before a project begins.

2. Professionalism
   Professionalism is crucial in all interactions, from initial consultations to project completion. Treat each client with respect, show up on time, and maintain a clean and organized work environment.

3. Patience and Empathy
   Clients may have questions, concerns, or even frustrations during the process. Being patient and empathetic helps clients feel heard and reassured, especially if they're facing unexpected challenges or delays.

4. Going Above and Beyond
   Small gestures, like following up after a project or offering extra tips, show clients that you genuinely care about their satisfaction. Going the extra mile can leave a lasting impression and increase the likelihood of positive reviews and referrals.

Implementing Customer Service Best Practices

Implementing best practices in customer service can improve client satisfaction and strengthen your business's reputation. Here's how to ensure your customer service meets high standards:

1. Train Your Team

If you have employees, train them in customer service skills, including effective communication, problem-solving, and professionalism. A well-trained team can ensure clients have a consistently positive experience.

2. Establish a Process for Managing Inquiries

Set up a process for responding to inquiries, such as a standard response time for emails and calls. Having a system in place ensures that clients receive timely, organized responses.

3. Listen Actively to Client Feedback

Active listening involves paying close attention to what clients are saying and confirming their needs and concerns. Listening carefully allows you to address their specific requirements and provides a better overall experience.

4. Create a Follow-Up Process

After completing a project, reach out to clients to thank them and ask if they have any additional questions or concerns. This follow-up shows your dedication to their satisfaction and reinforces your commitment to quality service.

Handling Client Concerns and Complaints

No business is immune to occasional complaints or issues, but handling them professionally can turn a negative situation into a positive outcome. Here's how to approach complaints and concerns effectively:

1. Acknowledge and Apologize

Acknowledge the client's concern and, if appropriate, offer a sincere apology. Showing empathy helps defuse tension and demonstrates that you're taking the issue seriously.

2. Understand the Problem Thoroughly

Ask questions to understand the issue fully before proposing a solution. This approach shows that you're committed to addressing their concern thoughtfully rather than offering a quick fix.

3. Provide a Solution and Timeline

Offer a clear solution and outline a timeline for addressing the problem. For example, if a client is unhappy with an installation detail, explain how you'll fix it and when they can expect completion.

4. Follow Up to Ensure Satisfaction

After resolving the issue, follow up with the client to confirm their satisfaction. This extra step demonstrates your commitment to service quality and ensures they feel valued.

Encouraging and Collecting Customer Feedback

Customer feedback provides valuable insights into how clients perceive your business and highlights areas for improvement. By actively encouraging and collecting feedback, you can identify strengths and address any weaknesses in your service.

1. Ask for Feedback at Project Completion

At the end of each project, ask clients for feedback on their experience. A simple question like, "Is there anything we could improve?" shows that you're open to constructive criticism.

2. Use Surveys for Detailed Insights

Sending a short survey via email can provide more structured feedback. Include questions about different aspects of the experience, such as responsiveness, professionalism, and quality of work.

3. Monitor Online Reviews

Regularly check online reviews on platforms like Google, Yelp, and Houzz. Respond to reviews, both positive and negative, to show that you value client opinions and are dedicated to service excellence.

4. Incorporate Feedback into Training

Use feedback to inform training and development. For instance, if several clients mention delays, work on improving project scheduling. Adjusting based on client feedback shows that you're committed to continuous improvement.

Maintaining Relationships After Project Completion

Staying connected with clients even after a project is completed can lead to repeat business and referrals. Here are ways to keep in touch with past clients:

1. Send Periodic Check-Ins

Sending occasional emails or postcards reminds clients of your services. A message like, "We hope you're enjoying your new floors! Let us know if there's anything we can do for you," keeps you top of mind.

2. Share Helpful Resources

Send clients seasonal maintenance tips or articles related to flooring care. Providing helpful information positions you as a resource and keeps the relationship active.

3. Offer Loyalty Discounts or Promotions

Encourage repeat business by offering discounts to past clients. A special promotion on refinishing services or a loyalty discount for referrals can incentivize clients to return.

Exceptional customer service is the foundation of long-lasting client relationships. By focusing on responsiveness, professionalism, and follow-through, you can create a client experience that builds loyalty, generates referrals, and strengthens your reputation in the flooring industry.

Leveraging Customer Loyalty Programs

A customer loyalty program can help retain existing clients by incentivizing repeat business and rewarding referrals. Loyalty programs encourage clients to choose your services over competitors and foster a sense of appreciation, making clients feel valued for their ongoing relationship with your business. This section explores different types of loyalty programs and how to implement one in your flooring business.

Types of Loyalty Programs

Loyalty programs come in various forms, allowing you to choose one that best suits your business and clients. Here are some popular types to consider:

1. Discount Programs for Repeat Services
   Offer discounts for clients who return for additional services, such as maintenance, refinishing, or upgrades. For example, you might provide a 10% discount on refinishing services if a client books within a year of installation.

2. Referral Rewards
   Encourage clients to refer your services by rewarding them for each successful referral. A discount, gift card, or credit toward future services can incentivize clients to spread the word.

3. Seasonal Promotions
   Run special seasonal promotions for loyal clients. For instance, offer a winter discount on refinishing or an autumn discount on maintenance services. This approach keeps clients engaged and encourages them to book services regularly.

4. Exclusive Access to New Products or Services
   Give loyal clients early access to new products, flooring materials, or services. Offering exclusivity creates a sense of privilege and appreciation, strengthening the client relationship.

Designing Your Loyalty Program

When designing a loyalty program, it's important to make it simple, valuable, and easy to understand. Here's how to develop a program that resonates with your clients:

1. Set Clear Rules and Rewards
   Define the specific rewards clients can earn and how they can achieve them. For example, "Refer a friend and receive 15% off your next service" or "Book a maintenance service within six months and get 10% off."

2. Choose a Reward System
   Decide whether rewards will be monetary (discounts or credits) or non-monetary (exclusive offers, thank-you gifts). Monetary rewards are generally straightforward, but non-monetary options can add a personal touch.

3. Promote the Program
   Clearly explain your loyalty program to clients during consultations, on your website, and in follow-up emails. Make sure clients understand the benefits and know how to participate.

4. Track Client Participation
   Use a tracking system to monitor who participates in the loyalty program and which rewards have been redeemed. A simple spreadsheet or customer relationship management (CRM) tool can help you manage this efficiently.

Communicating the Value of the Loyalty Program

Clients need to understand the benefits of your loyalty program to engage with it. Here's how to communicate its value:

1. Highlight Cost Savings
   Emphasize how clients can save money through the program, whether by booking maintenance services or referring friends. For example, "Save up to $200 on future projects by participating in our loyalty program!"

2. Showcase Exclusive Benefits

If you offer exclusive perks, such as access to premium products or priority scheduling, make sure clients know they're receiving something special for their loyalty.

3. Explain the Ease of Participation

Clients are more likely to join a program if it's easy to understand and access. Keep instructions simple and provide assistance if needed. A message like "Earn rewards just by booking your next service" can make it feel effortless.

Maintaining Engagement with Loyal Clients

Once clients join the program, regular engagement keeps them interested and aware of ongoing benefits. Here are some ways to maintain engagement:

1. Send Reminders About Rewards

Periodically remind clients about their available rewards or upcoming benefits. A quick email like, "Don't forget! You have 10% off your next service," helps keep the program top of mind.

2. Celebrate Milestones

Recognize client milestones, such as five referrals or three years of loyalty. Sending a small gift or thank-you message reinforces their value to your business.

3. Request Feedback on the Program

Ask clients for feedback on the loyalty program to see if they find it beneficial or have suggestions for improvement. This insight can help you tailor the program to better meet client needs.

Evaluating the Success of Your Loyalty Program

To ensure the program is effective, track key performance indicators (KPIs) that reflect its impact on client retention and satisfaction:

1. Participation Rate
Monitor how many clients are actively using the loyalty program. A high participation rate indicates that clients find the program valuable.

2. Repeat Business Rate
Measure the rate at which clients return for additional services. A successful loyalty program should contribute to a steady increase in repeat business.

3. Referral Rate
Track the number of referrals generated through the program. If referrals increase, your program is likely effective in encouraging word-of-mouth promotion.

4. Client Satisfaction
Gather feedback from participants to gauge satisfaction with the program. Positive feedback suggests that the program adds value, while constructive feedback can guide improvements.

A well-implemented loyalty program can enhance client satisfaction, encourage repeat business, and drive referrals. By creating a program that's simple, valuable, and engaging, you can foster long-term relationships that support steady growth for your flooring business.

Building a Reputation for Quality and Reliability

In the flooring industry, a reputation for quality and reliability is essential for attracting and retaining clients. When clients trust that you deliver high-quality work and adhere to timelines, they're more likely to choose your services over competitors. This section focuses on establishing and maintaining a reputation that clients can rely on, which is essential for fostering long-term relationships and generating referrals.

Delivering Consistent Quality

Providing consistently high-quality work is key to building trust with your clients. Here's how to ensure each project reflects the standards your business stands for:

1. Invest in Quality Materials

The materials you use play a significant role in the final outcome of a project. Partner with reliable suppliers and choose flooring products that meet client expectations for durability, appearance, and budget.

2. Hire Skilled Professionals

If you employ a team, invest in hiring skilled professionals who have experience in flooring installation and maintenance. Conduct regular training to ensure they understand the latest techniques and industry standards.

3. Maintain Attention to Detail

Pay attention to small details, such as alignment, finish, and cleanup. Small details can make a big difference in the final product and leave a lasting impression on clients.

4. Perform Quality Checks

Before considering a project complete, perform a thorough inspection to ensure every detail meets your standards. Conduct a final walk-through with the client to confirm they're satisfied with the work.

Communicating Reliability and Professionalism

Clients need to feel confident that your business is dependable. Demonstrate reliability and professionalism in every interaction to strengthen their trust:

1. Set Realistic Expectations

When discussing timelines, costs, and project scope, be realistic and transparent. Setting achievable expectations helps avoid misunderstandings and reinforces your commitment to honesty.

2. Show Up on Time

Timeliness is an important aspect of professionalism. Arriving on time for consultations, site visits, and project days demonstrates respect for the client's time and builds trust.

3. Meet Deadlines

Stick to the agreed-upon timeline whenever possible. If unexpected delays arise, communicate with the client immediately and provide an updated completion date.

4. Stay Organized

Organization helps projects run smoothly and minimizes errors. Use tools like project management software or a detailed schedule to keep track of each step and ensure timely completion.

Gathering and Showcasing Testimonials

Positive testimonials reinforce your reputation and build credibility with prospective clients. Here's how to gather and showcase testimonials effectively:

1. Request Testimonials After Each Project

After completing a project, ask satisfied clients if they'd be willing to provide a testimonial. Many clients are happy to share their experiences, especially if they're pleased with the results.

2. Make It Easy for Clients to Leave Reviews

Provide clear instructions on where and how to leave reviews, whether on your website, Google, Yelp, or Houzz. A simple follow-up email with a direct link to the review page can make the process easier.

3. Feature Testimonials on Your Website

Display testimonials prominently on your website, particularly on your homepage or a dedicated "Testimonials" page. Positive reviews give potential clients confidence in your services.

4. Use Testimonials in Marketing Materials

Incorporate client testimonials in your social media posts, brochures, and promotional emails. Testimonials add authenticity and show that real clients appreciate your work.

Leveraging Case Studies to Showcase Expertise

Case studies provide in-depth examples of past projects, demonstrating your expertise and approach to potential clients. They can also highlight specific challenges you overcame, showing clients that you're capable and resourceful. Here's how to develop and use case studies:

1. Choose Compelling Projects

Select projects that reflect a variety of services or unique challenges, such as custom installations, eco-friendly solutions, or complex refinishing. Diverse examples show that you're equipped to handle different types of flooring needs.

2. Highlight Client Goals and Outcomes

Start each case study by explaining the client's goals, followed by the approach you took to achieve them. Emphasize the results, such as improved aesthetics, durability, or added home value.

3. Include Before-and-After Photos

Visuals help clients understand the transformation you provided. Before-and-after photos illustrate the quality of your work and the impact it has on a space.

4. Use Case Studies in Proposals

Incorporate relevant case studies in proposals for new projects. Tailoring examples to each client's needs shows that you understand their unique requirements and can deliver results.

Monitoring and Managing Your Online Reputation

An online reputation is vital in today's digital landscape, where potential clients often research businesses before making decisions. Here's how to monitor and manage your online reputation effectively:

1. Set Up Alerts for Mentions
   Use tools like Google Alerts to monitor online mentions of your business. This allows you to stay informed about client feedback, media coverage, or mentions on social platforms.

2. Respond to Reviews, Both Positive and Negative
   Acknowledge positive reviews with a simple thank-you message. For negative reviews, respond professionally and offer solutions if appropriate. Handling criticism gracefully can reinforce trust.

3. Encourage Satisfied Clients to Share Their Experiences
   Politely encourage happy clients to leave online reviews. Remind them that their feedback helps other clients find reliable services and helps your business grow.

4. Address Common Concerns Publicly
   If you notice recurring issues or questions, address them publicly on your website or social media. Transparency shows that you value feedback and are proactive about improvement.

Building and maintaining a reputation for quality and reliability requires consistent effort, attention to detail, and a proactive approach to client satisfaction. By focusing on these principles, you'll foster long-term relationships, encourage referrals, and attract new clients to your flooring business.

The Power of Client Referrals and Word-of-Mouth Marketing

Word-of-mouth marketing and referrals are among the most powerful tools for business growth. When clients share positive experiences with others, it brings in new leads who are more likely to trust your services based on personal recommendations. This page delves into strategies for encouraging referrals and making word-of-mouth marketing a significant asset for your flooring business.

Why Referrals Matter

Client referrals offer several advantages:

1. Cost-Effective Marketing

Referral marketing requires little to no cost compared to traditional advertising. When clients refer friends, family, or colleagues, it's a powerful endorsement that doesn't require a large advertising budget.

2. Higher Conversion Rates

Potential clients referred by satisfied customers often convert more readily. Since they've already received positive feedback, they approach your business with trust and confidence.

3. Loyal Client Base

Clients who join through referrals tend to be more loyal and engaged, as they already have a personal connection to your business. This loyalty often translates into repeat business and further referrals.

Encouraging Client Referrals

To maximize referrals, it's essential to make the process easy and rewarding for clients. Here are strategies to encourage clients to refer your business to others:

1. Implement a Referral Program

Offer incentives for referrals, such as discounts, gift cards, or service credits. For example, you could offer a 10% discount on a future service for every successful referral or a small gift card as a token of appreciation.

2. Ask for Referrals Directly

Don't be afraid to ask happy clients for referrals. A simple statement like, "If you know anyone looking for flooring services, feel free to share our contact information," can remind clients to refer you.

3. Provide Business Cards or Referral Cards

Give clients a few business cards or referral cards to pass along to friends, family, or colleagues. Having a physical reminder makes it easy for clients to share your information.

4. Encourage Social Media Sharing

If clients are active on social media, encourage them to share their experience online. Positive posts about your work on platforms like Instagram, Facebook, or LinkedIn can reach a broader audience.

Creating a Memorable Client Experience

Clients are more likely to refer your business if they have an exceptional experience. Here's how to make each project memorable and encourage word-of-mouth promotion:

1. Deliver Outstanding Service

Exceed client expectations by providing high-quality work, clear communication, and a respectful, organized work environment. A great experience makes clients feel confident sharing your business with others.

2. Show Appreciation for Referrals

When a client provides a referral, thank them personally. A handwritten note, email, or small gift demonstrates your appreciation and encourages future referrals.

3. Keep in Touch

Regular follow-ups, seasonal greetings, or maintenance reminders help keep your business top of mind. Staying connected with past clients increases the likelihood of them referring you in the future.

Highlighting Referral Stories and Successes

Sharing referral stories and successes on your website or social media can encourage more clients to participate. Here are some ways to spotlight referrals:

1. Feature Client Testimonials

Highlight testimonials from clients who found you through referrals. Sharing these stories shows potential clients the positive impact of word-of-mouth marketing.

2. Share Referral Success Stories on Social Media
If a referral project turned out particularly well, share the story on social media with before-and-after photos, tagging or thanking the referring client if they're comfortable with it.

3. Create a "Client Spotlight" Feature
Consider creating a blog or social media feature that celebrates clients who refer others to your business. Recognizing clients for their support builds loyalty and encourages continued referrals.

Incentivizing Referrals Beyond Initial Projects

Encouraging referrals over the long term ensures a steady stream of new clients. Here's how to foster an ongoing referral network:

1. Offer Tiered Rewards for Multiple Referrals
Introduce rewards that grow with the number of referrals a client provides. For example, a client who refers three new clients might receive a larger discount or a gift.

2. Host Exclusive Events or Webinars
Invite loyal clients and their referrals to exclusive events, webinars, or workshops related to flooring, home renovation, or design. These events foster community and strengthen connections.

3. Provide a Referral Toolkit
Make it easy for clients to refer others by creating a referral toolkit, including business cards, brochures, and online resources they can share.

4. Encourage Reviews as Referrals
Online reviews serve as virtual referrals for new clients. Encourage satisfied clients to leave positive reviews on platforms like Google, Yelp, and Houzz to enhance your reputation.

Tracking and Measuring Referral Success

To assess the effectiveness of your referral strategy, track metrics that provide insights into the value of client referrals:

1. Number of Referrals per Client
   Track which clients have provided referrals and the number of referrals each client brings. This data helps identify top advocates and informs reward strategies.

2. Conversion Rate of Referred Clients
   Measure how many referred clients become paying customers. A high conversion rate indicates the success of your referral program and the trust clients have in your service.

3. Repeat Referral Rate
   Assess whether clients continue to refer others after their initial referrals. If clients consistently refer new business, it signals strong satisfaction and loyalty.

4. Revenue Generated from Referrals
   Calculate the total revenue generated from referred clients to understand the financial impact of word-of-mouth marketing. This information can help justify investments in a referral program.

A structured, client-centered approach to referral marketing can build trust, attract new clients, and deepen relationships with existing ones. By incentivizing referrals, creating memorable client experiences, and tracking success, you can harness the power of word-of-mouth marketing to support the long-term growth of your flooring business.

Chapter 6: Managing Finances for a Thriving Business

Financial management is a critical aspect of running a successful flooring business. Properly managing your finances ensures you have the resources to cover expenses, invest in growth, and build a stable future. This chapter explores financial fundamentals and offers strategies for organizing, tracking, and optimizing your business finances.

Why Financial Management Matters

Effective financial management helps you:

1. Maintain Positive Cash Flow
   Managing cash flow ensures you can cover day-to-day expenses, pay employees, and fund projects without stress. Positive cash flow is essential for stability and growth.

2. Plan for Growth
   By analyzing financial performance, you can identify areas where your business is thriving and reinvest profits into marketing, equipment, or expanding your team.

3. Build Resilience
   Strong finances enable you to handle unexpected costs, such as equipment repairs or project delays, without compromising business operations.

4. Ensure Tax Compliance
   Accurate financial records simplify tax preparation, helping you avoid penalties and reducing the risk of audits.

Setting Up a Business Bank Account

A dedicated business bank account separates personal and business finances, making it easier to track income, expenses, and tax obligations. Here's how to set one up:

1. Choose the Right Bank
   Research banks that offer business accounts with features tailored to small businesses, such as low fees, online banking, and access to business loans.

2. Organize Your Documentation
   To open a business account, you'll typically need your business license, EIN (Employer Identification Number), and proof of business ownership. Preparing these documents in advance speeds up the process.

3. Use the Account Exclusively for Business Transactions
   Once the account is open, ensure all income and expenses flow through

it. This practice simplifies financial tracking and demonstrates professionalism.

4. Consider Additional Accounts

Some businesses benefit from having separate accounts for savings, payroll, or taxes. Setting aside funds in a dedicated tax account, for example, ensures you're prepared for tax season.

Creating a Budget for Your Business

A budget provides a roadmap for your business finances, helping you allocate funds and control expenses. Here's how to create a realistic budget:

1. Estimate Monthly Income

Review historical sales data or estimate expected revenue based on your current client base. Use conservative estimates to avoid overspending.

2. List Fixed and Variable Expenses

Fixed expenses are regular costs, such as rent, utilities, and insurance. Variable expenses, like materials and fuel, fluctuate based on project volume. Include both to get a complete picture of your expenses.

3. Account for Seasonal Variations

Flooring businesses often have seasonal highs and lows. Factor in any expected revenue changes during slower months and allocate funds to cover those periods.

4. Allocate Funds for Savings and Growth

Set aside a percentage of income for savings and future investments. A growth fund can help you cover expansion costs, such as new equipment, marketing, or hiring.

Tracking and Analyzing Income and Expenses

Regularly tracking and analyzing income and expenses ensures you stay on top of your financial health. Here's how to organize your tracking process:

1. Use Accounting Software
   Tools like QuickBooks, FreshBooks, or Xero simplify tracking by automatically categorizing income and expenses. These programs also generate financial reports to aid decision-making.

2. Categorize Expenses
   Create categories for common expenses, such as materials, labor, rent, marketing, and utilities. Categorizing helps you identify where most of your income is going and highlights areas for potential savings.

3. Monitor Cash Flow Monthly
   Reviewing cash flow monthly allows you to spot trends and anticipate shortfalls. If a particular month shows a cash flow deficit, consider strategies to reduce expenses or delay non-urgent costs.

4. Reconcile Accounts Regularly
   Reconciling ensures that your records match your bank statements. Regular reconciliation catches discrepancies early and keeps your financial records accurate.

Understanding Profit and Loss Statements

A profit and loss (P&L) statement summarizes your revenue, expenses, and net profit over a specific period, typically monthly or quarterly. Here's how to use a P&L statement effectively:

1. Identify Key Revenue Sources
   Break down revenue by source, such as installation, repairs, and refinishing. Understanding which services generate the most income informs future business decisions.

2. Analyze Gross Profit
   Gross profit is your revenue minus the direct costs of goods sold (COGS), such as materials and labor. A healthy gross profit indicates that your pricing covers basic project costs.

3. Calculate Net Profit

Net profit is what's left after all expenses, including overhead and taxes, are deducted from your revenue. A positive net profit means your business is profitable; a negative figure signals a need to reduce expenses or increase revenue.

4. Use the P&L for Strategic Planning

Reviewing P&L statements regularly helps you spot financial trends. If profits decline over several months, investigate and adjust your pricing, marketing, or spending as needed.

Cash Flow Management Strategies

Cash flow is the lifeblood of any business. It refers to the money moving in and out of your business, and managing it effectively ensures you can cover expenses, pay employees, and invest in growth opportunities. This section explores strategies for maintaining a healthy cash flow, a vital aspect of financial stability and business success.

Why Cash Flow Management is Important

Maintaining positive cash flow helps your business remain stable, especially during leaner periods. Effective cash flow management:

1. Reduces Financial Stress

Knowing you have funds to cover immediate expenses reduces stress and improves decision-making.

2. Enables Timely Payments

Ensuring cash is available allows you to pay bills on time, maintain good vendor relationships, and avoid late fees.

3. Supports Business Growth

Positive cash flow enables you to reinvest in the business, whether through marketing, new hires, or updated equipment.

Strategies for Improving Cash Flow

Here are some strategies to improve cash flow and keep your flooring business financially healthy:

1. Negotiate Payment Terms with Vendors
   Speak with vendors about extending payment terms, such as net 45 or net 60, giving you more time to collect payments from clients before paying for materials.

2. Require Deposits for Large Projects
   For high-value projects, request an initial deposit to cover upfront expenses. Progress payments during the project also reduce financial strain, ensuring expenses are managed as the project progresses.

3. Incentivize Early Payments
   Offer small discounts to clients who pay their invoices early. A discount, even as low as 2% for early payments, can improve cash flow by encouraging clients to settle their bills quickly.

4. Use Invoice Factoring or Financing if Necessary
   If cash flow is tight, consider invoice factoring, where you sell outstanding invoices to a factoring company in exchange for immediate funds. Be mindful that this service typically comes with fees.

Projecting Cash Flow

Creating cash flow projections helps you anticipate future cash needs and avoid shortfalls. Here's how to create a simple cash flow projection:

1. List Expected Income for Each Month
   Estimate income from projects and other sources for each month. If your business has seasonal peaks, account for higher earnings during those months.

2. Account for Fixed and Variable Expenses
   Include regular expenses like rent and utilities as well as variable costs

related to project volume. If you expect any one-time expenses, factor them in as well.

3. Monitor Projected vs. Actual Cash Flow

Compare projections to actual cash flow monthly to identify discrepancies. If expenses consistently exceed projections, consider ways to cut costs or increase income.

4. Adjust Projections as Needed

Cash flow projections should be flexible. Adjust estimates based on recent performance, client payment patterns, or unexpected expenses.

Setting Up an Emergency Fund

An emergency fund provides a financial safety net for unexpected expenses, such as equipment repairs or seasonal slowdowns. Here's how to establish an emergency fund:

1. Determine an Initial Savings Goal

Start by setting aside enough to cover one month of operating expenses. As your business grows, aim to save enough to cover at least three to six months of expenses.

2. Automate Savings

Set up automated transfers to your emergency fund each month. Consistent contributions, even if small, build the fund over time.

3. Use Only for Genuine Emergencies

Limit the use of your emergency fund to true financial emergencies. This ensures it's available when you need it most, like during a project delay or unexpected downtime.

4. Replenish After Use

If you need to dip into the emergency fund, prioritize replenishing it as soon as cash flow improves. Maintaining the fund ensures you're always prepared.

Leveraging Business Credit

Business credit can be a valuable tool for managing cash flow, covering short-term expenses, or funding growth. Here's how to use business credit responsibly:

1. Establish Business Credit Early
   Open a business credit card or small line of credit to begin building your business credit score. This can help when applying for loans or larger lines of credit in the future.

2. Use Credit for Short-Term Expenses Only
   Avoid using credit to fund long-term expenses. Reserve it for short-term costs, like purchasing materials or covering a gap in cash flow that will soon be resolved.

3. Pay Off Balances Promptly
   Paying off credit balances on time not only avoids interest but also strengthens your credit score. A strong credit history can improve your chances of obtaining favorable financing terms in the future.

4. Monitor Your Credit Utilization Ratio
   Keep your credit utilization (the amount of credit used compared to available credit) below 30%. High utilization can negatively affect your credit score and limit future financing options.

Using Financial Metrics to Track Progress

Tracking financial metrics helps you measure the financial health of your business. Here are essential metrics to monitor regularly:

1. Gross Profit Margin
   Gross profit margin reflects profitability before overhead costs. Calculate it by dividing gross profit by total revenue. A high margin indicates efficient cost control and healthy pricing.

2. Operating Profit Margin
   Operating profit margin shows profitability after deducting operating

expenses. This metric indicates how efficiently your business operates relative to revenue.

3. Accounts Receivable Turnover

This ratio measures how often you collect outstanding invoices. A high turnover rate indicates effective collection practices, while a low rate suggests delays in receiving payments.

4. Current Ratio

The current ratio, or current assets divided by current liabilities, measures short-term financial health. A ratio above 1 indicates you can cover immediate obligations.

Effectively managing cash flow and monitoring financial metrics positions your flooring business for stability and growth. By forecasting cash flow, setting up an emergency fund, and using credit wisely, you can navigate financial challenges confidently and invest in opportunities as they arise.

Pricing Strategies for Profitability

Setting the right prices for your services is crucial for covering costs, generating profits, and staying competitive. This section explores different pricing strategies and how to implement them effectively, ensuring your flooring business remains both attractive to clients and profitable.

Understanding Pricing Basics

Your pricing needs to cover not only the direct costs of materials and labor but also overhead expenses like rent, utilities, and marketing. Here are some basics to consider when determining your pricing:

1. Direct Costs

These are the materials, labor, and other costs directly associated with each project. Accurately calculating these costs ensures your base price covers essential expenses.

2. Overhead Costs

Overhead includes expenses like office space, utilities, equipment maintenance, and administrative salaries. Factor these costs into your pricing to ensure your business remains sustainable.

3. Desired Profit Margin

The profit margin is the amount added to your base price to generate profit. Consider the level of profit you want to achieve based on industry standards, your expenses, and your business goals.

Types of Pricing Strategies

Different pricing strategies suit different business models and goals. Here are a few strategies commonly used in service-based businesses:

1. Cost-Plus Pricing

This method adds a set percentage (your profit margin) to the total cost of materials and labor. For example, if materials and labor cost $2,000 and you want a 20% margin, the price would be $2,400. This straightforward approach ensures all costs are covered and allows you to achieve a predictable profit.

2. Competitive Pricing

Competitive pricing involves setting prices based on what competitors charge. Research the local market to understand what similar businesses charge, then price your services in line with the competition or offer a slightly lower rate if you're building your client base.

3. Value-Based Pricing

With value-based pricing, you price your services according to the perceived value to the client rather than strictly based on costs. For high-end projects or unique flooring solutions, clients may be willing to pay more for quality or specialized skills.

4. Hourly Pricing

For projects with uncertain scope, such as complex repairs, you may choose an hourly rate rather than a flat project price. This approach ensures fair compensation for time and can be useful for tasks that vary widely in time requirements.

Setting Your Prices

Setting prices that balance profitability with competitiveness requires careful analysis. Here's how to set and refine your pricing:

1. Calculate Your Break-Even Point
   Determine the minimum price needed to cover costs without generating profit. This break-even point ensures you don't set prices too low to sustain the business.

2. Conduct Market Research
   Researching local competitors provides insight into market rates. Compare service offerings, quality, and reputation when evaluating pricing to ensure you're competitive without undervaluing your services.

3. Consider Client Demographics
   Tailor pricing to your target market's budget and expectations. For instance, higher-income neighborhoods may value premium options, while budget-conscious clients may appreciate straightforward, affordable pricing.

4. Test and Adjust Prices Periodically
   Test different prices to find what works best. Monitor client responses, project profitability, and market trends to adjust pricing as needed.

Presenting Your Prices to Clients

Clear communication around pricing helps clients understand the value of your services. Here's how to present pricing effectively:

1. Provide Detailed Estimates
   Break down estimates by itemizing labor, materials, and other charges. This transparency helps clients understand the pricing structure and reduces potential misunderstandings.

2. Highlight Value and Benefits
   Emphasize the quality of materials, expertise, and benefits your services offer. Showing clients the value they're getting makes them more comfortable with the price.

3. Offer Tiered Pricing Options
   For clients with varying budgets, consider offering good, better, and best options. Tiered pricing allows clients to choose a service level that meets their budget without compromising quality.

4. Explain Any Additional Fees
   If there are extra fees for travel, premium materials, or rush jobs, communicate them upfront. Being transparent about additional costs builds trust and prevents surprises.

Avoiding Common Pricing Mistakes

Setting prices too high or too low can impact profitability and client satisfaction. Here's how to avoid common pricing mistakes:

1. Underestimating Costs
   Failing to account for all costs can lead to underpricing. Ensure every expense, including indirect costs like administrative time, is factored into your calculations.

2. Ignoring Market Conditions
   Ignoring competitor pricing or client expectations can result in losing clients to competitors. Stay informed about market rates and trends to remain competitive.

3. Not Adjusting Prices for Inflation
   Over time, material costs, labor rates, and overhead increase. Periodically adjust prices to reflect these changes to avoid eroding profit margins.

4. Discounting Excessively

Offering too many discounts can devalue your services and hurt profitability. Use discounts strategically, such as for loyal clients or special promotions, rather than as a primary pricing tactic.

Evaluating Pricing Success

Regularly evaluating pricing ensures it aligns with your business goals and market conditions. Here's how to measure pricing effectiveness:

1. Calculate Profit Margins Regularly
   Review profit margins on completed projects to determine if prices are adequate. If margins are too low, consider adjusting prices or reducing costs.

2. Monitor Client Feedback on Pricing
   Client feedback can reveal whether clients feel they're receiving value for the price. Address concerns or confusion about pricing to improve client satisfaction.

3. Review Win/Loss Ratios
   The win/loss ratio reflects how often clients accept or decline your estimates. A high acceptance rate may indicate competitive pricing, while a low rate suggests prices may be too high.

4. Assess Revenue and Growth
   Regularly track revenue growth and financial performance. If revenue isn't meeting targets, examine whether pricing or client volume is contributing to the shortfall.

Implementing the right pricing strategy for your flooring business helps you stay profitable while meeting client expectations. By understanding costs, researching the market, and evaluating pricing regularly, you'll set prices that support growth and long-term success.

Budgeting for Growth and Scaling Your Business

Budgeting plays a pivotal role in managing resources effectively as you grow and scale your business. A solid growth budget not only supports day-to-day operations but also allocates resources to areas that drive expansion, such as marketing, hiring, and new equipment. This section explores strategies for creating a growth-focused budget to support a thriving flooring business.

Setting Financial Goals for Growth

Before budgeting for growth, establish clear financial goals. Here are common goals to consider:

1. Increasing Revenue
   Aim to increase revenue by a specific percentage over the next quarter or year. Identify which services, such as installation or repairs, have the most growth potential and focus on marketing these offerings.

2. Expanding Client Base
   Set a target for acquiring new clients each month. Consider the costs of client acquisition and determine how much you're willing to invest in marketing and outreach to reach this goal.

3. Upgrading Equipment
   If equipment or tools are outdated or need replacement, allocate part of the budget to updates. Reliable, high-quality tools improve efficiency, project quality, and employee satisfaction.

4. Building an Emergency Fund for Growth
   As your business grows, so should your emergency fund. Expanding your fund to cover three to six months of expenses ensures you can manage unexpected challenges during growth phases.

Allocating Resources to Key Areas of Growth

Effective growth budgeting involves allocating funds to the most impactful areas. Here's how to prioritize spending for business expansion:

1. Marketing and Advertising

Allocate a portion of your budget to marketing activities, including social media ads, local promotions, and networking events. Consider experimenting with various channels to see which yields the best return on investment (ROI).

2. Staffing and Training

If you plan to hire or need to expand your team, allocate funds for recruitment and onboarding. Additionally, set aside a budget for training current staff to improve skills and service quality.

3. Equipment and Technology

Budget for equipment upgrades or new technology that can enhance efficiency. For instance, investing in high-quality tools or flooring-specific software can streamline operations and improve client satisfaction.

4. Expansion to New Markets

If expanding geographically, allocate funds for market research, advertising in new locations, and the logistical costs associated with moving equipment or hiring local contractors.

Creating a Flexible Growth Budget

A growth budget needs flexibility to account for unexpected expenses and changes. Here's how to build adaptability into your budget:

1. Allocate a Contingency Fund

Set aside a portion of the budget as a contingency fund for unexpected expenses. Aim to reserve 5-10% of your total growth budget for unplanned needs.

2. Review and Adjust Quarterly

Revisit your budget quarterly to assess progress, review spending, and make adjustments. If certain areas are underperforming, reallocate funds to higher-impact areas.

3. Track Variable Costs Closely

Variable costs, such as project-specific materials and marketing expenses, can fluctuate. Monitor these costs regularly to identify trends and adjust spending as necessary.

4. Prepare for Seasonal Changes

Seasonal fluctuations can affect revenue and expenses. Allocate more resources during peak seasons and reduce spending during slower periods to ensure consistent cash flow.

Monitoring and Measuring Budget Performance

Measuring budget performance helps you understand which investments contribute most to growth and identify areas for improvement. Here's how to monitor growth budget performance:

1. Track ROI on Marketing Campaigns

Calculate ROI for each marketing campaign by comparing the cost of the campaign to the revenue it generates. Adjust marketing spend based on which channels deliver the highest returns.

2. Assess Staff Productivity and Efficiency

Evaluate how additional hires or training investments impact productivity. If you see improved project completion rates or client satisfaction, consider further investment in staffing.

3. Compare Budgeted vs. Actual Spending

Regularly compare your budget to actual spending to identify areas of overspending or underspending. Adjust future budgets based on these insights to optimize allocation.

4. Monitor Revenue Growth Rates

Track monthly and quarterly revenue growth to gauge the effectiveness of your growth investments. If revenue meets or exceeds targets, maintain or increase funding to successful areas.

Adjusting Your Growth Budget Based on Results

A successful growth budget requires ongoing adjustment. Here's how to refine your budget based on results:

1. Reallocate Funds to High-Performing Areas
If certain investments, like a specific marketing campaign, yield strong results, consider shifting more funds to similar initiatives. Focus on high-ROI activities that directly contribute to growth.

2. Reduce Spending in Low-Impact Areas
If certain budget areas aren't delivering results, consider reducing or reallocating those funds. Regularly review spending to ensure every dollar supports your growth goals.

3. Increase the Budget Gradually
As your business grows, increase your budget to support expanded operations. However, do this gradually to avoid overextending resources.

4. Seek Financial Advice as Needed
If managing growth becomes complex, consider consulting with a financial advisor or accountant. Expert guidance can help you make informed budgeting decisions and optimize resources effectively.

Budgeting for Sustainable Growth

Sustainable growth requires a budget that balances ambition with practicality. By strategically investing in marketing, staff, equipment, and new markets, you can expand your flooring business responsibly. Regularly assessing budget performance and adjusting based on results ensures your resources drive growth and support long-term success.

Preparing for Tax Season and Maintaining Financial Health

Proper tax planning and regular financial assessments are essential for maintaining the health of your flooring business. Staying compliant with tax regulations, organizing records, and planning for taxes in advance will save you time, reduce stress, and potentially lower your tax burden. This section offers guidance on preparing for tax season and managing your business finances throughout the year.

Organizing Financial Records

Accurate and organized records are key to tax preparation and compliance. Here's how to keep your financial records in order:

1. Maintain Separate Business Accounts
  Use a dedicated business bank account and credit card to keep personal and business finances separate. This simplifies record-keeping and provides clear documentation for expenses and income.

2. Categorize Expenses
  Set up categories for expenses like materials, labor, utilities, marketing, and travel. Organized categories streamline tax deductions and make it easier to identify spending patterns.

3. Save All Receipts and Invoices
  Keep all receipts and invoices, whether digital or physical, for at least seven years. Digital storage solutions like cloud services or accounting software can help you manage documents efficiently.

4. Use Accounting Software for Tracking
  Accounting software such as QuickBooks, FreshBooks, or Xero can help you track income, expenses, and generate reports. These tools simplify tax preparation and provide a clear view of your financial health.

Understanding Key Tax Deductions

Taking advantage of tax deductions can significantly reduce your taxable income. Common deductions for a flooring business may include:

1. Home Office Deduction
  If you work from home, you may qualify for a home office deduction. Calculate the square footage of your workspace as a percentage of your home's total area to determine the deductible portion.

2. Vehicle Expenses
  Deduct expenses related to business use of your vehicle, including fuel,

maintenance, and depreciation. Choose either the actual expense method or the standard mileage rate, whichever yields the higher deduction.

3. Supplies and Materials

Deduct the cost of materials, tools, and supplies used in projects. Keep detailed records to substantiate these expenses during tax filing.

4. Professional Services

Expenses for legal, accounting, or consulting services related to the business are deductible. This includes fees paid to financial advisors, business consultants, or other professional services.

5. Travel and Meals

Business-related travel, lodging, and meals are partially deductible. Ensure these expenses are documented, and keep receipts to justify business relevance if needed.

Setting Aside Funds for Taxes

Planning for taxes throughout the year helps prevent surprises during tax season. Here's how to prepare:

1. Estimate Quarterly Taxes

Small businesses typically pay estimated taxes quarterly. Use the previous year's tax liability as a guide, or consult with an accountant to estimate payments accurately.

2. Set Aside a Percentage of Income

Designate a portion of each payment received for taxes. Many business owners set aside around 20-30% of their income, but consult with a tax professional to determine the exact percentage.

3. Open a Dedicated Tax Account

Consider opening a separate savings account solely for tax funds. Transferring tax reserves into this account keeps the money accessible and earmarked specifically for tax obligations.

4. Review and Adjust Annually

Tax laws change, so review your tax strategy yearly. Consult with an accountant to adjust estimates, optimize deductions, and plan for changes in tax regulations.

Preparing for Filing and Avoiding Penalties

Preparing for tax filing in advance helps reduce the risk of errors or penalties. Here are steps to ensure smooth filing:

1. Organize Documents Early

Begin gathering documents, such as bank statements, receipts, and invoices, early in the tax season. Organizing ahead of time reduces last-minute stress and allows you to verify information.

2. Review for Accuracy

Ensure all entries are accurate and double-check totals for income, expenses, and deductions. Accurate reporting minimizes the risk of IRS scrutiny and penalties.

3. File on Time or Request Extensions

File taxes by the deadline or request an extension if you need more time. Filing late without an extension may result in penalties or interest charges.

4. Work with a Qualified Tax Professional

A tax professional familiar with small business taxes can ensure compliance, identify deductions, and offer strategic advice. Working with an expert helps you make the most of your tax filings and avoid common mistakes.

Regular Financial Health Checkups

Periodic financial assessments help you identify trends, set goals, and improve your business's financial health. Here's how to maintain financial wellness year-round:

1. Review Financial Statements Quarterly

Examine profit and loss statements, balance sheets, and cash flow statements each quarter. Regular reviews help you understand your financial position and guide strategic decisions.

2. Monitor Profitability Metrics

Track key metrics like gross profit margin, net profit margin, and expense ratios. Monitoring these metrics over time shows how effectively your business operates and where to improve.

3. Adjust the Budget as Needed

If revenue or expenses deviate from projections, adjust your budget accordingly. A flexible budget helps you stay on track financially, even as business conditions change.

4. Plan for Future Investments

Consider setting aside funds for future investments, like equipment upgrades, expansion, or hiring. Proactively planning for growth keeps your business agile and ready to seize new opportunities.

Establishing Long-Term Financial Goals

Set goals that promote long-term stability and growth. Consider goals like building a retirement fund, saving for a larger office space, or expanding services. Regularly reviewing and adjusting these goals ensures they align with your vision and current business performance.

By preparing for taxes, maintaining organized records, and assessing financial health regularly, you set your flooring business up for success. Sound financial management helps you meet obligations, reduce stress, and focus on growing a prosperous, sustainable business.

Chapter 7: Building a Strong Team

The Importance of a Skilled and Reliable Team

A successful flooring business relies on more than just high-quality materials and equipment; it requires a skilled and dependable team. A strong team ensures projects run smoothly, maintains a positive work environment, and upholds the quality standards that define your brand. This chapter explores the importance of building an effective team and offers strategies for recruiting, training, and retaining skilled employees.

Benefits of a Strong Team

Building a capable team provides several advantages, such as:

1. Enhanced Productivity
   A skilled team can complete tasks more efficiently, reducing project timelines and increasing the number of jobs you can take on, which ultimately boosts revenue.

2. Consistent Quality
   Trained employees who understand your standards deliver consistent, high-quality work, which reinforces your business's reputation and

ensures client satisfaction.

3. Increased Client Trust

Clients feel more confident hiring a business with experienced, professional employees. This trust can lead to repeat clients, referrals, and positive reviews.

4. Reduced Turnover Costs

Retaining skilled employees reduces the costs associated with hiring, training, and onboarding new staff, saving time and resources in the long run.

Recruiting Skilled Employees

Finding the right talent for your flooring business is essential for maintaining high standards. Here are some strategies to attract qualified candidates:

1. Define Clear Job Descriptions

A well-defined job description helps attract candidates with the right skills and experience. Outline specific duties, required qualifications, and any physical demands, such as lifting heavy materials or working on various flooring types.

2. Advertise Through Industry Channels

Post job openings on industry-specific job boards, local trade schools, and flooring associations. These channels reach candidates with relevant skills and experience.

3. Offer Competitive Compensation

To attract skilled workers, research market rates and offer competitive wages. Benefits such as health insurance, paid time off, and bonuses for quality work or client satisfaction can also make your business more appealing.

4. Provide Opportunities for Growth

Skilled workers seek positions with advancement potential. Highlight any opportunities for promotion, skill-building, or additional certifications that you support.

Conducting Effective Interviews

A structured interview process helps identify candidates who align with your business's goals and values. Here's how to conduct effective interviews:

1. Ask About Relevant Experience
   Inquire about previous flooring work, including types of materials used, specific skills, and familiarity with tools and equipment. Experience with different flooring types—such as hardwood, tile, or carpet—may be beneficial.

2. Assess Problem-Solving Abilities
   Ask situational questions that gauge how candidates handle challenges, such as dealing with a material shortage or addressing client concerns. Problem-solving skills are crucial for fieldwork and client satisfaction.

3. Evaluate Communication Skills
   Good communication ensures smooth teamwork and effective client interactions. Observe how clearly candidates express themselves, especially when discussing technical topics or past projects.

4. Discuss Work Ethic and Reliability
   Consistency and reliability are vital in meeting project deadlines. Ask candidates about their attendance history, punctuality, and approach to handling workload pressures.

Onboarding New Team Members

A structured onboarding process ensures new hires are prepared and aligns them with your company's expectations. Here's how to create a smooth onboarding experience:

1. Introduce Company Values and Standards
   Begin onboarding by explaining your company's mission, values, and

standards for quality. Clear expectations from the start ensure new employees understand your commitment to excellence.

2. Provide Job-Specific Training

Depending on their experience level, new hires may need training on specific tools, materials, or techniques. Pair them with experienced employees for hands-on learning and guidance.

3. Emphasize Safety Protocols

Flooring work involves physical labor and potential hazards. Ensure new hires are familiar with safety procedures, including using protective gear and handling materials correctly.

4. Encourage Questions and Feedback

Create an open environment where new hires feel comfortable asking questions. Feedback from new team members can also provide insights into improving onboarding and training processes.

Creating a Positive Work Culture

A supportive work culture fosters loyalty, job satisfaction, and productivity. Here's how to cultivate a positive environment for your team:

1. Recognize Employee Contributions

Acknowledge the hard work of your team members, whether through verbal praise, employee-of-the-month awards, or performance bonuses. Recognition motivates employees to maintain high standards.

2. Encourage Collaboration and Teamwork

Promote a sense of camaraderie by encouraging teamwork and cooperation on projects. Team-building activities, such as regular meetings or after-work gatherings, build rapport among employees.

3. Provide Open Communication Channels

Ensure employees feel comfortable sharing ideas, concerns, or feedback. An open-door policy or regular check-ins with team members creates a transparent and inclusive work environment.

4. Support Work-Life Balance
   Respect employees' time off and personal commitments. A balanced schedule promotes well-being, reduces burnout, and leads to greater job satisfaction.

Setting Long-Term Goals for Team Development

Establishing long-term goals for team growth encourages skill development and aligns your team with your business objectives. Here's how to set effective goals:

1. Offer Skill-Building Opportunities
   Invest in ongoing training for employees, whether through workshops, certifications, or trade events. Skill-building benefits both individual employees and the overall quality of work.

2. Encourage Leadership Development
   Identify team members with leadership potential and provide opportunities for them to lead projects, train new hires, or take on additional responsibilities.

3. Set Performance Benchmarks
   Establish measurable benchmarks for individual and team performance, such as client satisfaction ratings, project completion times, or accuracy. Regularly review progress and provide feedback.

4. Reward Consistent Improvement
   Recognize employees who consistently improve their skills or exceed performance expectations. Acknowledging growth motivates the team and fosters a culture of excellence.

A skilled, motivated team is a valuable asset that enhances client satisfaction, productivity, and overall business growth. By recruiting the right talent, providing effective training, and fostering a positive work culture, you'll build a team that supports the success and reputation of your flooring business.

Recruiting and Retaining Top Talent

Attracting and retaining skilled employees is essential for a thriving business. A stable team of dedicated employees ensures that projects run smoothly and that quality remains consistent, reinforcing your company's reputation. This section focuses on strategies for recruiting top talent and fostering a positive work environment to improve retention.

Finding Qualified Candidates

Finding the right employees for your business begins with sourcing candidates who have the skills, attitude, and reliability needed for success. Here's how to reach potential employees:

1. Build Relationships with Trade Schools and Training Centers
 Partnering with trade schools and vocational centers can connect you with recent graduates skilled in flooring and construction. Many institutions offer job placement services to help students find employment in their fields.

2. Leverage Online Job Boards and Professional Networks
 Online platforms such as Indeed, LinkedIn, and industry-specific job boards provide access to a large pool of candidates. Make sure to post detailed job descriptions that accurately represent the skills and experience required.

3. Encourage Employee Referrals
 Current employees can be an excellent source of referrals, as they likely know others in the trade. Offer referral incentives to employees who bring in qualified candidates who are eventually hired.

4. Highlight Company Culture in Job Listings
 Job seekers are often drawn to companies with strong, supportive cultures. Include information about your company's values, team atmosphere, and growth opportunities in job postings to attract

like-minded candidates.

Creating a Competitive Compensation Package

Competitive compensation is a major factor in attracting and retaining skilled employees. Here's how to design an appealing package:

1. Offer Fair Wages Based on Market Rates
   Research local and industry salary data to ensure your wages are competitive. Competitive pay demonstrates respect for your employees' skills and effort, which enhances job satisfaction.

2. Provide Health and Retirement Benefits
   Benefits like health insurance and retirement plans, even if basic, make a position more attractive. If full benefits aren't feasible, consider offering perks such as flexible hours, performance bonuses, or paid time off.

3. Incorporate Performance-Based Bonuses
   Rewarding employees for outstanding work or meeting performance goals can boost motivation and productivity. Bonuses tied to client satisfaction, project quality, or efficiency encourage employees to excel.

4. Cover Costs for Certification and Skill Development
   Employees value opportunities to grow professionally. Offer to cover costs for certifications or skill-development courses, which can also enhance the quality of work they bring to your business.

Onboarding for Long-Term Success

An effective onboarding process introduces new hires to the business and prepares them for success in their roles. Here's how to structure onboarding for optimal results:

1. Introduce New Hires to Key Team Members
   Assign a mentor or buddy who can show new employees the ropes and introduce them to other team members. Building connections early helps

new hires feel welcomed and part of the team.

2. Provide Comprehensive Training

A structured training program covers all essential aspects of the job, from safety protocols to technical skills. Hands-on training with experienced employees ensures new hires gain confidence in their roles.

3. Set Clear Expectations from Day One

Provide an overview of your company's expectations regarding attendance, quality standards, and client interactions. Transparency from the beginning reduces misunderstandings and aligns new hires with company goals.

4. Regularly Check in During the First 90 Days

Schedule periodic check-ins during the first few months to discuss progress, answer questions, and address any concerns. Ongoing support demonstrates your investment in their success.

Fostering a Culture of Engagement and Loyalty

A positive work culture promotes loyalty, reduces turnover, and helps employees feel valued. Here's how to cultivate engagement and encourage long-term commitment:

1. Promote Open Communication

Encourage employees to voice their ideas, suggestions, and concerns. Regular team meetings and an open-door policy create an inclusive environment where employees feel heard.

2. Show Appreciation for Hard Work

Recognize employees for their contributions, whether through verbal praise, recognition programs, or small rewards. Acknowledgment fosters a sense of pride and motivates employees to continue performing well.

3. Create Opportunities for Team Bonding

Organize team-building activities, such as group outings, casual lunches, or after-work events, to foster camaraderie. Strong relationships among team members improve collaboration on projects.

4. Encourage a Healthy Work-Life Balance
   Avoid overworking employees by maintaining reasonable hours and respecting time off. A balanced schedule enhances well-being, reduces burnout, and contributes to higher retention.

Investing in Ongoing Employee Development

Ongoing development helps employees build skills, improves morale, and strengthens your business's expertise. Here are ways to support continued learning and growth:

1. Offer Regular Training Opportunities
   Provide access to workshops, webinars, or seminars on topics relevant to flooring, safety, or customer service. Ongoing training helps employees stay updated on industry trends and best practices.

2. Encourage Cross-Training Among Team Members
   Cross-training allows employees to learn different roles within the business, providing flexibility and enhancing team cohesion. Employees who understand various roles are better equipped to support one another.

3. Set Individual Growth Goals
   Work with employees to establish personal growth goals, such as learning a new skill or taking on a leadership role. Regular progress reviews show employees that their growth is valued and supported.

4. Reward Skill Improvement and Initiative
   Recognize employees who take initiative to develop their skills or improve performance. Providing rewards for personal growth reinforces a culture of continuous improvement.

Managing Team Performance

Maintaining high standards for performance is essential for a successful business. Here's how to monitor and support team performance effectively:

1. Conduct Regular Performance Reviews
   Hold formal reviews periodically to discuss strengths, areas for improvement, and career aspirations. Use these discussions to reinforce positive behaviors and address any performance issues constructively.

2. Set Clear, Measurable Goals
   Provide each team member with specific, measurable goals aligned with the company's objectives. Clear goals give employees direction and a sense of accomplishment when achieved.

3. Address Performance Issues Promptly
   If performance falls short, address concerns respectfully and provide guidance for improvement. Clear, honest feedback helps employees adjust and improves the overall team dynamic.

4. Celebrate Milestones and Successes
   Recognize individual and team achievements, whether it's completing a challenging project or reaching a business milestone. Celebrating successes boosts morale and fosters a sense of team unity.

Creating a team of skilled, motivated employees requires dedication to recruitment, training, and retention. By investing in your team's success and fostering a positive work culture, you'll build a loyal, capable team that drives your flooring business toward growth and excellence.

Developing Leadership Skills Within Your Team

Encouraging leadership skills within your team can enhance productivity, strengthen team morale, and prepare your business for growth. When team members have the opportunity to develop leadership abilities, they become more invested in the business, take on additional responsibilities, and contribute to a positive work culture. This section provides strategies for identifying and nurturing leadership potential within your team.

Identifying Potential Leaders

Recognizing individuals with leadership potential is the first step in building a team of future leaders. Here's how to spot qualities that signal strong leadership skills:

1. Strong Communication Skills
   Effective leaders communicate clearly, listen actively, and can convey information in a way that inspires and motivates others. Look for employees who naturally explain processes well or offer constructive feedback to peers.

2. Problem-Solving Abilities
   Leaders are quick to identify and address issues, whether it's resolving a scheduling conflict or addressing a client concern. Team members who proactively seek solutions demonstrate the problem-solving mindset of a leader.

3. Accountability and Reliability
   Those who consistently meet deadlines, produce quality work, and take responsibility for their actions show accountability. This reliability is crucial for leadership, as it builds trust within the team.

4. A Willingness to Learn
   Leaders are committed to continuous growth. Employees who seek out learning opportunities, attend workshops, or ask questions to improve their skills display a desire for personal development.

Creating Leadership Development Opportunities

Providing development opportunities empowers team members to build essential leadership skills. Here are some ways to nurture potential leaders:

1. Assign Responsibility for Smaller Projects
   Start by giving potential leaders responsibility over smaller projects or specific tasks. This allows them to experience decision-making and

accountability on a manageable scale.

2. Encourage Mentorship Roles
Pair experienced team members with newer employees in a mentorship role. Mentorship fosters leadership skills by encouraging team members to share knowledge, provide guidance, and model professional behavior.

3. Involve Team Members in Planning
When planning projects, encourage team members to participate in the process. Their involvement fosters ownership and hones skills in strategic thinking and project coordination.

4. Promote Cross-Functional Training
Provide opportunities for employees to train in different roles within the business. Exposure to various aspects of the operation gives them a holistic understanding of the business and enhances leadership versatility.

Supporting Leadership Development with Training

Structured training programs reinforce leadership skills and prepare team members for future responsibilities. Here's how to support leadership training effectively:

1. Offer Leadership Workshops and Seminars
Invest in workshops that cover topics such as communication, conflict resolution, and decision-making. These skills are invaluable in any leadership role and build confidence in emerging leaders.

2. Provide Access to Online Courses
Online courses on platforms like Coursera, LinkedIn Learning, and Udemy offer leadership training that employees can complete at their own pace. Encourage team members to pursue relevant courses and discuss takeaways with them.

3. Host Internal Leadership Development Sessions
Lead internal training sessions on leadership topics relevant to your

business. For instance, a session on "Effective Client Communication" can prepare team members to represent the company in a professional manner.

4. Encourage Self-Directed Learning
Recommend books, articles, and videos on leadership. Self-directed learning encourages team members to take initiative and deepen their understanding of effective leadership practices.

Promoting a Culture of Collaboration and Trust

A strong leader promotes collaboration, trust, and respect among team members. Here's how to create an environment that encourages these values:

1. Encourage Open Dialogue Among Team Members
Promote an atmosphere where team members feel comfortable sharing ideas and concerns. Leaders who foster open dialogue create a collaborative and supportive team culture.

2. Empower Team Members to Make Decisions
Giving team members the autonomy to make decisions on smaller matters builds confidence and trust. When they feel empowered, they're more likely to take initiative and contribute positively.

3. Model Ethical and Respectful Behavior
Leaders should model integrity, respect, and professionalism. Encourage employees to lead by example, demonstrating qualities that inspire others to follow their lead.

4. Celebrate Team Successes
Recognize team achievements and milestones, whether it's completing a challenging project or receiving positive client feedback. Celebrating successes reinforces teamwork and fosters loyalty.

Evaluating Leadership Progress and Providing Feedback

Regular feedback supports continuous growth and improvement for emerging leaders. Here's how to assess and support their leadership journey:

1. Conduct Periodic Check-Ins
   Schedule one-on-one meetings with employees in leadership development to discuss progress, address challenges, and provide feedback on their leadership approach.

2. Set Clear, Achievable Goals
   Work with potential leaders to set specific, measurable goals related to their development. Clear goals, such as improving communication skills or leading a small project, provide direction and motivation.

3. Provide Constructive Feedback
   Offer feedback that highlights strengths and identifies areas for improvement. Encourage leaders to reflect on feedback and integrate it into their daily interactions and responsibilities.

4. Celebrate Milestones in Development
   Acknowledge progress by celebrating milestones in their leadership journey. Recognizing growth reinforces positive behaviors and encourages continued development.

Aligning Leadership Development with Business Goals

Effective leaders align their actions with the company's mission and objectives. Here's how to ensure that leadership development supports business goals:

1. Incorporate Business Values in Training
   Reinforce core business values—such as quality, reliability, and client satisfaction—throughout leadership training. Team members should understand how these values influence decision-making and leadership actions.

2. Communicate Company Objectives Clearly
   Help potential leaders understand how their contributions and

leadership development support the company's long-term goals. Clear communication fosters a sense of purpose and alignment.

3. Encourage Strategic Thinking
   Encourage leaders to think strategically about their projects, considering how their decisions impact both short- and long-term goals. Strategic thinking prepares leaders for future challenges and growth.

4. Foster Accountability to Company Standards
   Encourage team members to hold themselves and others accountable to company standards, reinforcing consistency in quality and professionalism.

Developing leaders within your flooring business creates a team capable of driving growth, maintaining quality, and supporting each other's success. By identifying leadership potential, offering growth opportunities, and aligning leadership development with your business goals, you can build a strong, adaptable team that enhances your business's reputation and long-term success.

Creating a Culture of Accountability and Excellence

Establishing a culture of accountability and excellence is essential for fostering a team that consistently meets high standards. When team members understand the importance of accountability and are encouraged to pursue excellence, they contribute positively to the company's reputation and client satisfaction. This section outlines strategies for cultivating these values within your team.

Encouraging Accountability in Daily Work

Accountability means that each team member takes ownership of their actions, meets commitments, and strives to uphold the company's standards. Here's how to encourage accountability:

1. Set Clear Expectations and Responsibilities
   Clearly define each team member's role and responsibilities to avoid

confusion and ensure they know what's expected of them. Detailed job descriptions and regular updates on expectations help maintain accountability.

2. Establish Deadlines and Milestones

Setting deadlines and milestones for tasks keeps projects on track and helps team members stay focused. Regularly check progress and celebrate completed milestones to reinforce the importance of meeting goals.

3. Promote Transparency in Work Processes

Encourage team members to be transparent about challenges or delays. Open communication allows managers to address issues early, support team members, and keep projects on track.

4. Implement a System for Tracking Performance

Use tools or software to track each team member's progress and performance. Regular performance tracking makes it easy to identify areas for improvement and recognize employees who consistently meet expectations.

Fostering a Commitment to Excellence

Excellence goes beyond meeting minimum requirements; it means continually striving to deliver high-quality work. Here's how to inspire a commitment to excellence:

1. Lead by Example

As a leader, model excellence in your own work. Demonstrate attention to detail, professionalism, and a strong work ethic, showing team members the standards you expect.

2. Encourage Continuous Learning

Provide resources and opportunities for skill development, such as workshops, certifications, or industry events. When team members improve their skills, they're better equipped to perform at a high level.

3. Emphasize the Value of Quality Work

Reinforce the importance of quality work by recognizing team members who go above and beyond. Highlight the impact of excellence on client satisfaction and the company's reputation.

4. Set High Standards and Provide Constructive Feedback
Set clear quality standards for projects, and provide constructive feedback when standards aren't met. Constructive feedback helps team members understand how to improve and encourages a proactive approach to excellence.

Building Trust and Mutual Respect Among Team Members

Trust and respect are essential for a positive work environment where team members feel valued and motivated. Here's how to cultivate these values:

1. Encourage Open Communication and Listening
Foster an environment where team members feel comfortable sharing ideas, feedback, and concerns. Encourage active listening to ensure everyone feels heard and respected.

2. Acknowledge and Celebrate Individual Strengths
Recognize each team member's unique strengths and contributions. Celebrating individual talents builds mutual respect and appreciation within the team.

3. Handle Conflicts with Fairness and Respect
Address conflicts quickly and fairly, focusing on solutions rather than assigning blame. Handling conflicts respectfully reinforces trust and shows that each team member's perspective is valued.

4. Support Team-Building Activities
Plan team-building activities to strengthen connections among team members. Whether through regular meetings, workshops, or social events, team-building fosters trust and cooperation.

Implementing Regular Feedback Loops

Regular feedback provides team members with insights into their performance and areas for improvement. Here's how to establish effective feedback processes:

1. Conduct Routine Performance Reviews
   Hold formal reviews quarterly or annually to discuss performance, achievements, and development opportunities. Use these sessions to recognize progress and set future goals.

2. Encourage Peer Feedback
   Create opportunities for team members to give each other constructive feedback. Peer feedback highlights strengths and areas for improvement from those who work closely with each other.

3. Provide Real-Time Feedback
   Offer feedback on the spot for specific actions or tasks, whether positive or corrective. Real-time feedback is immediate and actionable, helping team members make quick improvements.

4. Encourage Self-Reflection and Goal Setting
   Ask team members to reflect on their own performance and set personal goals for improvement. Self-reflection fosters accountability and personal growth.

Recognizing and Rewarding Accountability and Excellence

Rewarding accountability and excellence reinforces these values and motivates team members to maintain high standards. Here's how to recognize and celebrate these qualities:

1. Acknowledge Achievements Publicly
   Recognize accomplishments in team meetings, newsletters, or internal communications. Public recognition shows that accountability and excellence are valued across the organization.

2. Offer Incentives for High Performance
   Provide bonuses, paid time off, or other rewards for outstanding

performance. Financial incentives motivate employees to consistently deliver high-quality work.

3. Create an Employee of the Month Program
Implement an Employee of the Month program to recognize team members who demonstrate accountability and excellence. Highlighting their efforts encourages others to strive for similar achievements.

4. Celebrate Team Successes as Milestones
When the entire team meets a major goal or completes a challenging project, celebrate together. Celebrations can be as simple as a team lunch or a recognition event, fostering camaraderie and reinforcing a collective commitment to excellence.

Aligning Accountability and Excellence with Business Goals

Ensuring that accountability and excellence align with your business objectives strengthens the company's mission and reputation. Here's how to connect these values with your business goals:

1. Integrate Values into Performance Metrics
Include accountability and excellence as criteria in performance evaluations. Making these values part of performance metrics emphasizes their importance and impact on business goals.

2. Reinforce Company Standards Regularly
Remind team members of the company's standards and expectations in meetings and training sessions. Consistent reinforcement ensures everyone is aligned with the business's mission.

3. Tie Individual and Team Goals to Company Objectives
Align individual performance goals with broader business objectives, such as client satisfaction or project efficiency. Clear alignment makes it easier for team members to see how their work contributes to the company's success.

4. Evaluate Progress Toward Business Goals

Regularly review how well the team's accountability and commitment to excellence support the company's goals. Use these assessments to adjust strategies and keep everyone aligned.

Building a team culture grounded in accountability and excellence supports client satisfaction, enhances productivity, and strengthens your company's reputation. By setting clear expectations, promoting continuous improvement, and recognizing achievements, you'll foster a motivated, high-performing team that consistently upholds your business's standards.

Retaining Top Talent and Planning for Future Team Growth

Retaining skilled team members and planning for future growth are essential for long-term business success. High retention rates reduce hiring costs, increase productivity, and build a cohesive, reliable team. This section covers strategies to retain top talent and create a scalable plan for future team growth, helping your flooring business maintain stability as it expands.

Understanding the Importance of Employee Retention

Retaining top talent provides several benefits, including:

1. Reduced Hiring and Training Costs
   High turnover requires frequent recruiting and training, which can be costly and time-consuming. Retaining skilled employees minimizes these expenses.

2. Enhanced Team Morale and Cohesion
   A stable team builds strong relationships and a shared commitment to company goals, enhancing team morale and cohesion.

3. Higher Productivity
   Experienced employees work more efficiently, complete projects faster, and contribute to higher productivity than constantly training new hires.

4. Improved Client Satisfaction

Clients appreciate working with familiar, experienced team members who understand the company's values and quality standards.

Strategies for Retaining Skilled Employees

Here are some effective strategies to help you retain skilled employees:

1. Provide Competitive Benefits
Offer benefits that matter to employees, such as health insurance, paid time off, or retirement plans. Even small benefits demonstrate that you value their well-being.

2. Encourage Career Development
Support employees' professional growth by offering skill development opportunities, promotions, and leadership roles. When employees see a clear career path, they're more likely to stay with the company.

3. Foster a Positive Work Environment
Cultivate a supportive, inclusive culture where employees feel respected and valued. A positive work environment boosts job satisfaction and reduces turnover.

4. Maintain Open Communication
Regularly check in with employees to address concerns, gather feedback, and show appreciation. Open communication builds trust and strengthens the employee-manager relationship.

Recognizing and Rewarding Long-Term Employees

Recognizing the loyalty and dedication of long-term employees reinforces their commitment and motivates others. Here's how to show appreciation for their contributions:

1. Celebrate Work Anniversaries
Acknowledge employees' work anniversaries with personalized messages, certificates, or small gifts. Celebrating milestones shows that you value their dedication.

2. Offer Loyalty Bonuses

Consider offering bonuses or incentives for employees who reach significant milestones, such as five, ten, or fifteen years with the company. Loyalty bonuses encourage long-term commitment.

3. Highlight Achievements Publicly

Recognize employees' accomplishments in team meetings or newsletters. Public acknowledgment reinforces their value within the team and inspires others.

4. Encourage Long-Term Goals

Support employees in setting and pursuing long-term career goals within the company. Help them develop a clear path for advancement that aligns with your business goals.

Planning for Future Team Expansion

Planning for growth ensures that you're prepared to expand your team when the time comes. Here's how to develop a scalable plan for future team growth:

1. Evaluate Team Needs Periodically

Regularly assess your team's capacity, workload, and skills to determine whether expansion is necessary. Periodic evaluations allow you to plan ahead for future hiring needs.

2. Identify Key Roles for Expansion

Identify roles that will be essential for future growth, such as project managers, client coordinators, or specialized technicians. Knowing which roles to fill helps streamline the hiring process.

3. Prepare for Seasonal and Project-Based Hiring

Some flooring businesses experience seasonal demand fluctuations. Plan for temporary or project-based hires to handle peak workloads without overextending resources.

4. Build a Talent Pipeline

Establish relationships with trade schools, industry networks, and online job boards to build a pipeline of qualified candidates. A talent pipeline ensures you have access to potential hires when expansion is needed.

Creating a Growth-Friendly Company Culture

As your team grows, maintaining a positive company culture becomes essential for stability. Here's how to preserve your culture as you expand:

1. Reinforce Core Values During Growth
   Continuously communicate and reinforce core company values, such as quality, integrity, and teamwork. Core values provide a foundation that aligns new hires with the existing team.

2. Encourage Inclusivity and Diversity
   Strive for a diverse, inclusive workforce where team members feel valued regardless of background. Inclusivity strengthens morale and creates a more dynamic team.

3. Promote Team Cohesion
   Facilitate team bonding through meetings, social events, and collaborative projects. A cohesive team adapts better to growth and works more effectively together.

4. Adapt Leadership to Scale
   As the team grows, consider establishing team leaders or department heads to manage specific areas. Leadership roles within the team help streamline communication and maintain quality as the business expands.

Developing a Long-Term Succession Plan

A succession plan ensures that critical roles within the company are filled seamlessly, preserving continuity and stability. Here's how to create a succession plan for your business:

1. Identify Key Positions and Skills
   Determine which roles are vital to your business's success and the skills required for those positions. Identifying key roles helps you plan for transitions in case of promotions, retirements, or departures.

2. Cultivate Potential Successors
   Train and mentor employees who demonstrate potential to take on leadership roles. Preparing successors internally fosters continuity and reduces the need for external hiring.

3. Document Processes and Procedures
   Ensure that critical processes and tasks are documented. This documentation serves as a reference for successors, enabling them to transition smoothly into their new roles.

4. Regularly Review and Update the Plan
   Periodically review and update your succession plan to reflect any changes in business goals, team structure, or skills needed for key roles.

Regularly evaluating retention and growth efforts allows you to make adjustments and improve outcomes. Here's how to assess the impact of these strategies:

1. Track Retention Rates
   Monitor employee turnover and retention rates to gauge the success of your retention strategies. Low turnover rates indicate effective retention practices, while high turnover signals areas for improvement.

2. Collect Employee Feedback on Growth Initiatives
   Solicit feedback from employees regarding growth initiatives, career development, and satisfaction with the company culture. Their input provides insights into the effectiveness of your strategies.

3. Measure Team Productivity and Client Satisfaction
   Evaluate productivity and client satisfaction to assess how well the team performs as it grows. High productivity and client satisfaction suggest that growth and retention efforts are supporting business goals.

4. Adjust Strategies Based on Findings

Use your findings to refine retention and growth strategies. Regular adjustments ensure that your team remains strong, cohesive, and aligned with your business objectives.

A well-planned approach to employee retention and team growth ensures that your business remains resilient, productive, and prepared for future success. By investing in your team's development, recognizing loyalty, and planning for expansion, you'll cultivate a skilled, committed workforce that supports the business as it grows and adapts to new challenges.

Chapter 8: Navigating Challenges and Building Resilience

Identifying and Understanding Common Challenges

Running a flooring business comes with unique challenges, from managing client expectations to dealing with unforeseen circumstances. This chapter explores common challenges in the flooring industry and strategies for building resilience to overcome them effectively.

Understanding Industry-Specific Challenges

Awareness of industry-specific challenges prepares you to address them proactively. Here's an overview of common issues faced by flooring businesses:

1. Fluctuating Material Costs
   Prices for flooring materials like wood, tile, and carpet can vary based on market demand and supply chain factors. These fluctuations affect project costs and can reduce profit margins if not managed carefully.

2. Labor Shortages and Skill Gaps
   Finding skilled labor in the flooring industry can be difficult, especially during busy seasons. Labor shortages impact project timelines and may compromise quality if the team is overextended.

3. Supply Chain Delays
Delays in receiving materials due to supply chain issues can halt projects and lead to client dissatisfaction. A reliable supply chain is essential for maintaining project timelines.

4. Seasonal Variations in Demand
Flooring businesses may experience seasonal fluctuations in demand, with busy periods around home renovation seasons and slower months in between. Understanding these cycles helps with planning and budgeting.

Developing Problem-Solving Skills and Adaptability

Problem-solving skills enable you to address issues as they arise and maintain business continuity. Here's how to build a problem-solving mindset:

1. Practice Root Cause Analysis
When a challenge arises, identify its root cause rather than just addressing symptoms. Understanding the core issue allows for more effective, long-term solutions.

2. Consider Multiple Solutions
Brainstorm several potential solutions for each problem. Evaluating options promotes flexibility and increases the likelihood of finding the best approach.

3. Learn from Past Challenges
Reflect on past issues and how they were handled. Lessons learned from previous challenges help prepare for future situations and inform better decision-making.

4. Encourage Creative Thinking Among Team Members
Foster an environment where team members feel comfortable suggesting innovative solutions. Collaborative problem-solving leads to diverse ideas and often more effective solutions.

Managing Client Expectations Effectively

Clear communication with clients helps set realistic expectations and prevents misunderstandings. Here's how to manage client expectations proactively:

1. Set Clear Project Timelines
   Provide clients with an estimated timeline that accounts for potential delays. Clearly communicating timelines prevents surprises and fosters understanding if challenges arise.

2. Be Transparent About Material Choices
   Explain material options, availability, and associated costs to clients. Transparency in material discussions helps clients make informed decisions and reduces potential conflicts.

3. Address Budget Constraints Early
   Discuss budget expectations with clients during initial consultations. A realistic budget discussion minimizes misunderstandings and allows for accurate planning.

4. Provide Regular Updates Throughout the Project
   Keep clients informed of project progress and any changes to the timeline or budget. Regular updates maintain trust and demonstrate professionalism.

Building a Reliable Network of Suppliers and Partners

A dependable network of suppliers and partners is invaluable during challenges. Here's how to build and maintain a strong network:

1. Establish Relationships with Multiple Suppliers
   Having multiple suppliers reduces dependency on a single source and mitigates risks associated with supply chain delays.

2. Communicate Regularly with Key Partners
   Keep open lines of communication with suppliers, subcontractors, and

other partners. Strong relationships make it easier to resolve issues and negotiate during challenging times.

3. Seek Partners with Flexible Payment Terms
Work with suppliers who offer flexible payment terms, such as credit or delayed payment options. Flexible terms support cash flow and provide financial relief during tight periods.

4. Prioritize Reliable Partners During Selection
Choose partners who demonstrate reliability and professionalism. A trustworthy network ensures you have support when faced with supply chain disruptions or other challenges.

Preparing for Unforeseen Circumstances

Proactive planning prepares your business to handle unexpected situations. Here's how to develop a plan for unforeseen circumstances:

1. Create an Emergency Fund
Set aside a portion of profits to create a cash reserve for emergencies. An emergency fund provides a financial cushion during unexpected challenges.

2. Develop Contingency Plans for Key Projects
Identify critical points in each project where delays may occur and plan alternative actions. Contingency plans reduce downtime and keep projects on track.

3. Regularly Review Insurance Coverage
Ensure your business insurance covers all potential risks, such as liability, equipment, and property damage. Comprehensive coverage reduces financial risk.

4. Train Team Members on Crisis Management
Prepare your team to respond to crises, such as material shortages or safety incidents. Crisis management training ensures everyone knows how to handle unexpected situations calmly.

By understanding industry challenges, managing client expectations, and preparing for the unexpected, you'll build a resilient flooring business that can weather setbacks. Proactive planning, clear communication, and a reliable network empower your business to thrive despite challenges and position you for long-term success.

Enhancing Financial Stability During Challenging Times

Financial resilience is critical for navigating tough periods and keeping your flooring business on solid ground. This section outlines strategies for managing cash flow, reducing expenses, and sustaining profitability through economic ups and downs.

Strengthening Cash Flow Management

Managing cash flow effectively ensures that your business can cover expenses and invest in growth, even during slow periods. Here's how to improve cash flow stability:

1. Track Inflows and Outflows Rigorously
   Monitor income and expenses weekly or monthly to understand your cash position. Regular tracking highlights patterns, helps you anticipate challenges, and supports proactive decision-making.

2. Prioritize Accounts Receivable
   Encourage prompt payment by setting clear payment terms and following up on outstanding invoices. Offering small discounts for early payments can also improve cash flow.

3. Delay Non-Essential Expenses
   Postpone purchases or investments that are not immediately necessary during slow periods. Delaying non-essential expenses frees up funds for more urgent needs.

4. Build a Cash Reserve for Slow Months
   Set aside a portion of revenue each month to create a buffer for slower

periods. A cash reserve helps cover expenses without resorting to loans or credit during challenging times.

Optimizing Operating Costs

Streamlining expenses without sacrificing quality helps maintain profitability. Here's how to optimize operating costs:

1. Negotiate Better Terms with Suppliers
   Reach out to suppliers to negotiate favorable terms, such as discounts for bulk orders or extended payment periods. Lower costs improve cash flow and reduce financial strain.

2. Reduce Utility and Overhead Costs
   Implement energy-saving practices and reduce waste in your operations. Small changes, like using energy-efficient lighting or reducing material waste, can lower utility bills.

3. Evaluate Subscription Services and Contracts
   Review recurring expenses, such as software subscriptions or service contracts, to determine if they're essential. Cancel or downgrade non-essential services to reduce costs.

4. Leverage Bulk Purchasing and Discounts
   Buy materials in bulk when possible to take advantage of lower unit costs. Bulk purchasing saves money in the long run and ensures that materials are readily available.

Exploring Alternative Revenue Streams

Diversifying income sources stabilizes revenue and reduces dependency on specific services. Here's how to explore additional revenue options:

1. Offer Maintenance and Repair Services
   Maintenance and repair services provide recurring income and help fill slower periods. Regular clients often value these additional services as part of an ongoing relationship.

2. Introduce Seasonal Promotions and Packages

Create seasonal offers, such as spring cleanings or holiday preparation services, to attract clients during slow seasons. Promotions bring in additional revenue and keep your team active.

3. Consider Online Consultations or Classes

If feasible, offer virtual consultations or classes on flooring care, maintenance, or design. These services expand your client base beyond your local area and generate extra income.

4. Sell DIY Kits or Guides for Minor Repairs

For minor flooring repairs, consider selling DIY kits or instructional guides. These products appeal to clients who enjoy hands-on projects and add a passive revenue stream to your business.

Preparing for Economic Downturns

Economic downturns are challenging for many businesses, but strategic preparation improves resilience. Here's how to prepare for and manage during tough economic times:

1. Monitor Economic Indicators and Industry Trends

Stay informed about economic trends and forecasts in your industry. Understanding trends helps you anticipate changes and adapt your strategy to market conditions.

2. Focus on High-Margin Services

Prioritize services with higher profit margins, such as custom installations or premium material options, during slower economic periods. High-margin services boost profitability when demand is lower.

3. Expand Clientele to Include Commercial Contracts

If your business focuses mainly on residential clients, consider pursuing commercial contracts. Commercial projects can provide steady income and diversify your client base.

4. Increase Client Retention Efforts

Strengthen relationships with current clients through loyalty programs, follow-ups, and personalized service. Satisfied clients are more likely to return, helping to maintain revenue.

Building Strong Relationships with Financial Partners

Having a positive relationship with financial partners, such as banks or lenders, provides support during tough times. Here's how to build and maintain these relationships:

1. Establish a Line of Credit Before It's Needed
   Set up a line of credit while your business is stable. A credit line provides quick access to funds during emergencies without the need for new loan applications.

2. Maintain Open Communication with Lenders
   Keep your bank or lender informed about your business's performance. Regular updates create trust and can lead to favorable terms if you need additional financing.

3. Explore Financing Options for Growth or Survival
   Consider options like SBA loans, equipment financing, or invoice factoring during downturns. Financing can support cash flow, allowing you to continue operations without depleting reserves.

4. Seek Financial Advice and Support
   Consult a financial advisor to evaluate your business's financial health and develop strategies for economic challenges. Expert guidance ensures well-informed decisions that support long-term stability.

By enhancing cash flow management, exploring new revenue streams, and preparing for economic challenges, you'll strengthen your flooring business's financial resilience. A proactive approach to financial stability ensures that your business remains viable and adaptable, no matter the economic climate.

Enhancing Team Resilience in Times of Change

Building a resilient team capable of adapting to change strengthens your business's ability to handle challenges. This section covers strategies for fostering adaptability, maintaining motivation, and supporting team members during times of uncertainty.

Encouraging Adaptability Among Team Members

A team that embraces adaptability is better equipped to handle unexpected changes. Here's how to cultivate adaptability within your team:

1. Foster a Growth Mindset
   Encourage a mindset focused on learning and improvement. Celebrate team members who embrace challenges and view setbacks as learning opportunities.

2. Offer Training in New Skills
   Provide training sessions for skills relevant to evolving industry needs, such as working with new materials or learning improved installation techniques. Skill-building keeps your team agile.

3. Implement Flexible Work Practices
   When possible, offer flexible scheduling or cross-train team members for various roles. Flexibility enhances team adaptability and reduces disruptions during transitions.

4. Encourage Open Communication About Changes
   Create an environment where team members feel comfortable discussing upcoming changes. Open dialogue minimizes resistance and prepares team members for adjustments.

Maintaining Team Motivation During Challenging Times

Keeping your team motivated, especially during tough periods, helps sustain productivity and morale. Here's how to support team motivation:

1. Set Clear, Achievable Goals
   Break down larger objectives into manageable goals. Clear goals provide direction and give team members a sense of accomplishment when reached.

2. Recognize and Celebrate Small Wins
   Acknowledge milestones and celebrate achievements, no matter how small. Celebrations remind the team of their progress and reinforce positive contributions.

3. Provide Encouragement and Support
   Offer encouragement and check in regularly with team members, especially when challenges arise. A supportive attitude demonstrates leadership and boosts morale.

4. Encourage Team Involvement in Problem-Solving
   Involve the team in developing solutions to challenges they're experiencing. Participation in problem-solving fosters ownership and investment in the business's success.

Supporting Mental and Emotional Well-being

A resilient team is one that feels supported, both mentally and emotionally. Here's how to prioritize your team's well-being:

1. Promote Work-Life Balance
   Encourage reasonable working hours and respect team members' personal time. Work-life balance reduces burnout and promotes long-term job satisfaction.

2. Provide Access to Mental Health Resources
   If possible, offer resources like counseling services or wellness programs. Supporting mental health shows you value team members' overall well-being.

3. Encourage Taking Breaks and Time Off

Allow and encourage regular breaks and time off. Rest and recovery are essential for maintaining energy and focus during challenging periods.

4. Listen and Be Approachable

Maintain an open-door policy and encourage team members to share concerns. Being approachable helps team members feel heard and respected.

Building Team Unity Through Shared Goals

A unified team is more resilient and better able to face challenges together. Here's how to strengthen unity through shared goals:

1. Involve the Team in Setting Goals

Allow team members to contribute to goal-setting, especially for projects that directly impact their work. Involvement fosters buy-in and shared responsibility.

2. Encourage Collaborative Problem-Solving

Encourage teamwork in addressing issues and finding solutions. Collaborative problem-solving strengthens bonds and builds trust among team members.

3. Hold Regular Team Meetings for Updates

Regular meetings provide opportunities for updates, discussion, and support. Meetings reinforce a sense of unity and keep everyone aligned with business goals.

4. Celebrate Successes Together

When the business reaches a milestone or achieves success, celebrate as a team. Shared celebrations reinforce team spirit and recognize collective efforts.

Developing Leadership Skills to Guide the Team

Effective leadership provides stability and guidance during periods of change. Here's how to enhance your leadership skills to support a resilient team:

1. Lead by Example During Challenging Times
   Demonstrate resilience, adaptability, and positivity, especially during tough situations. Leading by example inspires team members to follow suit.

2. Communicate Vision and Purpose
   Regularly communicate the business's vision and goals to the team. A clear sense of purpose keeps the team focused and motivated, even during uncertainty.

3. Practice Empathy and Understanding
   Show empathy toward team members facing personal or professional challenges. Understanding their experiences fosters trust and a supportive environment.

4. Encourage Professional Development
   Support team members' growth through professional development opportunities, such as training or workshops. Investing in their skills benefits both the team and the business.

By fostering adaptability, supporting well-being, and building a strong team culture, you'll create a resilient team capable of facing industry challenges and adapting to change. A supportive, motivated, and unified team becomes a foundation for long-term success and stability in your flooring business.

Managing Risk and Ensuring Business Continuity

Risk management is essential to safeguarding your business from potential setbacks and ensuring it can continue operating smoothly during difficult times. This section explores strategies for identifying risks, creating contingency plans, and maintaining continuity during disruptions.

Identifying Potential Risks in Operations

Understanding potential risks in your business allows you to address them before they become major issues. Here's how to identify key risks in flooring operations:

1. Assess Common Operational Risks
   Evaluate risks related to material availability, labor shortages, equipment reliability, and project delays. Identifying common risks helps prepare for issues you're likely to encounter.

2. Consider Financial and Economic Risks
   Analyze risks associated with cash flow fluctuations, economic downturns, and market demand changes. Financial risk management ensures you have resources to weather economic changes.

3. Evaluate Legal and Regulatory Risks
   Stay informed about laws related to business licensing, contracts, and workplace safety. Understanding legal obligations prevents potential penalties or disputes.

4. Include Environmental and Safety Risks
   Identify risks related to workplace safety and environmental factors, such as hazardous materials or extreme weather. Preparing for these risks minimizes health hazards and project delays.

Developing a Comprehensive Risk Management Plan

A risk management plan prepares your business to handle unexpected events and maintain continuity. Here's how to create an effective plan:

1. Prioritize Risks Based on Impact and Likelihood
   Rank risks by their potential impact on your business and likelihood of occurrence. Prioritizing risks helps allocate resources to the most critical areas.

2. Establish Mitigation Strategies for High-Priority Risks
   Develop strategies to reduce the likelihood or impact of high-priority risks. For instance, building relationships with multiple suppliers can

mitigate the impact of supply chain issues.

3. Assign Responsibilities for Risk Management
Designate team members responsible for monitoring specific risks, such as safety officers for workplace hazards. Clear responsibilities ensure quick responses to emerging issues.

4. Review and Update the Risk Plan Regularly
Regularly review and update the plan to adapt to new risks or changes in business operations. A dynamic plan keeps risk management relevant and effective.

Creating Contingency Plans for Business Continuity

Contingency plans outline steps to keep your business operational during disruptions. Here's how to prepare continuity strategies for common scenarios:

1. Develop Plans for Material or Supply Shortages
Identify alternative suppliers or materials that can substitute in case of shortages. Contingency plans for materials ensure projects can continue with minimal interruption.

2. Prepare for Potential Labor Shortages
Cross-train employees and maintain relationships with reliable contractors. Cross-training increases flexibility, while a contractor network provides backup labor.

3. Establish Financial Backup Options
Set up a business line of credit or maintain emergency savings to cover expenses during disruptions. Financial reserves support cash flow and keep the business stable.

4. Create Communication Protocols for Emergencies
Develop a communication plan to inform clients and team members during disruptions. Clear, timely communication minimizes confusion and maintains trust.

Investing in Insurance for Risk Mitigation

Insurance is a critical component of risk management, protecting your business from major financial losses. Here's how to evaluate and choose the right insurance options:

1. Evaluate Liability Insurance for Client Protection
   Liability insurance covers damages if your business causes property damage or client injury. Coverage reassures clients and protects your business from costly claims.

2. Consider Workers' Compensation for Employee Safety
   Workers' compensation provides financial support for employees injured on the job. This coverage meets legal requirements and fosters a safe work environment.

3. Explore Business Interruption Insurance
   Business interruption insurance covers lost income if you're unable to operate due to certain events, such as natural disasters. This policy protects revenue during forced closures.

4. Consult with an Insurance Professional
   Work with an insurance agent to assess coverage options suited to your business's specific risks. Professional guidance ensures you choose policies that align with your needs.

Preparing for Crisis Management

Crisis management plans prepare your team to handle unexpected events calmly and efficiently. Here's how to develop effective crisis response protocols:

1. Develop a Crisis Management Team
   Assign a team responsible for managing crises, including roles such as communication lead and safety officer. A dedicated team coordinates actions and prevents chaos.

2. Create Crisis Response Checklists

For each potential crisis, develop checklists outlining specific actions to take. Checklists provide clear instructions, helping team members respond quickly and effectively.

3. Conduct Regular Crisis Drills and Training

Hold drills for scenarios like evacuation, equipment failure, or severe weather. Regular practice ensures everyone knows their role and builds confidence in crisis response.

4. Review Crisis Plans After Each Incident

After any crisis, review what worked well and what needs improvement. Continuous improvement makes your crisis management stronger and more effective over time.

By proactively managing risks, preparing contingency plans, and investing in comprehensive insurance, your flooring business will be better equipped to handle disruptions and continue operations. Effective risk management and crisis preparedness safeguard your business's long-term resilience, ensuring stability even in challenging times.

Evaluating and Learning from Challenges

Reflecting on past challenges and evaluating the effectiveness of your responses helps build resilience for future obstacles. This section discusses how to assess outcomes, gather insights, and implement improvements based on lessons learned.

Conducting Post-Challenge Evaluations

After facing a challenge, a thorough evaluation provides clarity on what worked well and what can be improved. Here's how to conduct an effective evaluation:

1. Analyze the Root Causes of the Challenge

Identify the underlying factors that contributed to the issue, whether it was supply chain delays, team shortages, or client expectations. Understanding the root cause enables targeted improvements.

2. Assess the Effectiveness of Your Response

Evaluate how your team responded to the challenge, including communication, decision-making, and actions taken. Determine which responses were successful and where improvements are needed.

3. Gather Feedback from Team Members

Involve your team in the evaluation process to get their perspective. Team members may have insights about specific aspects of the response that could be improved.

4. Document Findings for Future Reference

Create a record of each evaluation, including details about the challenge, response, and lessons learned. Documenting insights helps prepare for similar issues in the future.

Implementing Process Improvements

Based on your evaluation, implement changes to strengthen your operations and prevent similar challenges from recurring. Here's how to make effective process improvements:

1. Adjust Procedures to Address Weaknesses

Modify any procedures or workflows that may have contributed to the issue. For example, adjust project timelines or sourcing methods if delays were a problem.

2. Provide Additional Training as Needed

If skills gaps were identified, provide targeted training to improve team readiness. Training keeps your team prepared to handle similar situations effectively.

3. Enhance Communication Protocols

Strengthen communication protocols if misunderstandings or delays in information-sharing contributed to the challenge. Clear communication ensures faster, coordinated responses.

4. Set Up Early Warning Systems
   Create systems or processes to detect issues before they escalate, such as regular supply checks or client check-ins. Early detection allows for proactive adjustments.

Establishing a Culture of Continuous Improvement

A culture focused on learning and improvement helps your business stay adaptable and resilient. Here's how to foster a culture of continuous improvement within your team:

1. Encourage Open Dialogue on Challenges
   Create an environment where team members feel comfortable discussing challenges and potential improvements. Open dialogue promotes transparency and collaborative problem-solving.

2. Celebrate Learning and Growth
   Recognize team members who contribute ideas for improvement or excel in challenging situations. Celebrating growth reinforces a positive, proactive mindset.

3. Incorporate Feedback Loops into Operations
   Regularly gather feedback on processes, especially after completing projects. Continuous feedback ensures ongoing improvements and keeps standards high.

4. Set Regular Review Intervals for Policies
   Schedule periodic reviews of operational policies to ensure they remain effective. Regular reviews keep processes aligned with current needs and industry standards.

Learning from Industry Trends and Innovations

Staying informed about industry trends and advancements can reveal new ways to approach challenges. Here's how to leverage industry knowledge for resilience:

1. Attend Industry Conferences and Workshops
Conferences and workshops offer insights into emerging trends, tools, and best practices. Staying updated allows you to adopt improvements that benefit your business.

2. Follow Industry Publications and Thought Leaders
Industry publications and thought leaders provide valuable information on challenges and solutions. Regular reading keeps you informed and inspired.

3. Network with Other Professionals
Connect with other professionals in your industry to share experiences and learn from each other's strategies. Networking fosters knowledge-sharing and provides diverse perspectives.

4. Invest in Innovative Tools and Technologies
Consider adopting tools or technologies that streamline operations, such as project management software or advanced installation equipment. Innovations improve efficiency and preparedness.

Preparing for Future Challenges

Using lessons from past challenges to prepare for future scenarios strengthens your business's resilience. Here's how to incorporate lessons learned into future planning:

1. Develop Scenario-Based Training
Use past challenges as scenarios for team training. Scenario-based training prepares team members for similar situations and reinforces effective response strategies.

2. Create a Risk Management Checklist
Based on prior experiences, create a checklist of common risks and preventive measures. A checklist provides a quick reference during planning and keeps risks top-of-mind.

3. Set Up a Response Toolkit
   Assemble tools, contact lists, and resources needed for common challenges, such as a list of backup suppliers or contact information for support services. A toolkit ensures you're ready to respond quickly.

4. Review Lessons Learned Periodically
   Revisit documented lessons from past challenges on a regular basis. Reviewing insights reinforces learning and keeps your team prepared for potential issues.

By evaluating and learning from each challenge, you'll continuously strengthen your flooring business's resilience. A proactive approach to improvement and a focus on industry innovation position your business to adapt effectively to future challenges, ensuring long-term stability and growth.

Chapter 9: Dealing with Competition in the Flooring Business

Understanding Your Competition

In the flooring industry, competition can be intense. Knowing who your competitors are and understanding their strengths and weaknesses is essential for positioning your business to stand out. This section covers strategies for identifying and analyzing your competitors, helping you leverage insights for a competitive edge.

Identifying Local and Regional Competitors

To effectively compete, you need a clear picture of who you're up against. Start by identifying other flooring companies in your area, including local businesses and regional chains. Take note of their services, specialties, target clients, and pricing structures. Ask yourself the following questions:
- What types of flooring do they specialize in (e.g., hardwood, laminate, tile)?
- Who is their target audience? Residential, commercial, or both?
- Are their services limited to specific neighborhoods, or do they operate regionally?

Understanding the competitive landscape at both local and regional levels allows you to see where your business fits and identify market gaps you could fill.

Analyzing Competitors' Strengths and Weaknesses

After identifying your competitors, analyze their strengths and weaknesses. Competitor analysis helps you understand why clients might choose their services over yours and vice versa. Here are some common strengths to look for:
- Pricing: Do they offer low-cost options that appeal to budget-conscious clients?
- Specialty Services: Are there services, like custom flooring design, that they excel in?
- Reputation: What do their online reviews reveal about client satisfaction?

Similarly, examine areas where they might lack. Perhaps their customer service is subpar, or they don't offer high-quality products. Weaknesses represent opportunities for you to excel, allowing your business to offer value that competitors do not.

Learning from Competitor Successes and Failures

Studying your competitors' successes and failures provides valuable insights into what resonates with clients and what doesn't. For example, analyze:
- Marketing Techniques: Note the advertisements and promotions that competitors use and how well they engage clients.
- Customer Reviews and Feedback: Explore online reviews to understand common complaints or praised aspects, as they highlight client expectations and service gaps.
- Service Approach: Consider whether they focus on specific materials, client education, or post-project follow-up, and evaluate how these approaches affect client satisfaction.

Learning from your competitors' experiences equips you with practical knowledge on how to improve your offerings and avoid potential pitfalls. This understanding positions your business to adapt quickly to client needs and stand out within a competitive market.

Building a Competitive Advantage

To stand out in the flooring industry, your business needs a distinct edge. By establishing a competitive advantage, you can capture clients' attention and loyalty, making your services the preferred choice in a crowded market. This section focuses on defining and promoting your unique selling points, offering specialized services, and enhancing customer satisfaction.

Defining Your Unique Selling Points (USPs)

Your unique selling points (USPs) are the distinguishing factors that make your flooring business preferable to competitors. Identifying and promoting these aspects helps potential clients see what makes your business exceptional. Examples of effective USPs in the flooring industry include:
- Eco-Friendly Materials and Practices: Offering sustainable and environmentally friendly flooring options is increasingly appealing to conscious consumers.
- Fast Installation Services: For clients seeking minimal disruption, emphasizing your quick and efficient installation can be a major draw.
- High-Quality Craftsmanship and Expertise: Highlight the skill level and experience of your team, especially if you have certifications or specialize in a particular flooring type.

Once identified, promote your USPs consistently across marketing materials, social media, and during consultations. Emphasizing these unique elements will differentiate your business from others.

Providing Superior Customer Service

In the service industry, customer care is a critical component of success. Providing a high standard of customer service can set your flooring

business apart from competitors, even those with similar products and pricing. Here's how to build a strong reputation for customer care:
- Listen and Respond to Client Needs: Understand each client's preferences, timelines, and budget constraints. Personalizing service increases client satisfaction and builds loyalty.
- Transparent Communication: Keep clients updated throughout the project, from material selection to installation. Clear communication prevents misunderstandings and boosts trust.
- Resolve Issues Quickly and Professionally: Address any concerns or complaints immediately. Clients appreciate responsiveness and feel valued when issues are resolved efficiently.

Exceptional customer service enhances the client experience and leads to positive reviews and word-of-mouth referrals, both powerful tools for competing in a crowded market.

Offering Specialized Services

Specialized services allow your business to cater to niche markets and differentiate itself from competitors who may only provide standard offerings. Here are examples of specialized services that can attract new clients:
- Custom Design and Installation: Offering unique, personalized flooring designs or custom inlays can appeal to clients who want a one-of-a-kind result.
- Repair and Restoration Services: Not every flooring business offers repair or restoration. Providing this service attracts clients looking to maintain or restore existing flooring.
- Post-Installation Maintenance Packages: Offer clients an option for regular maintenance after installation. Maintenance packages can add value and encourage long-term relationships.

By positioning your business as a specialist in certain services, you can reach clients who prioritize expertise and quality over standard options.

Strengthening Customer Loyalty

In a competitive industry, loyal clients are invaluable. Cultivating strong client relationships not only encourages repeat business but also drives referrals and enhances your reputation. This section explores ways to foster customer loyalty through loyalty programs, follow-ups, and referral incentives.

Creating a Loyalty Program

Loyalty programs reward clients for choosing your services, making them more likely to return and recommend your business to others. Here are a few ways to create an effective loyalty program for your flooring business:
- Discounts for Repeat Clients: Offer a discount on future projects for clients who return, showing appreciation for their loyalty.
- Exclusive Benefits for Returning Clients: Provide perks such as priority scheduling or complimentary consultations for loyal customers.
- Points-Based Rewards System: For each purchase, clients can earn points that can be redeemed for services, products, or discounts on future projects.

A well-designed loyalty program can give your business a significant edge by incentivizing repeat business and boosting customer satisfaction.

Following Up After Each Project

Following up with clients after project completion shows that you value their satisfaction, even after the transaction. This level of care is memorable and can lead to stronger client relationships. Here are some effective follow-up practices:
- Post-Project Surveys or Calls: Gather feedback on their experience, both to improve your services and to make clients feel heard.
- Maintenance Tips or Care Instructions: Providing helpful information on flooring maintenance keeps clients connected and reassures them of your commitment to quality.

- Seasonal or Yearly Check-Ins: Checking in periodically to see if clients need any additional services or maintenance keeps your business top of mind.

Regular follow-ups are a simple way to show clients that your service doesn't end once the project is complete. This helps in creating a lasting positive impression.

Encouraging Referrals

Referrals are one of the most effective forms of marketing in a service-based industry like flooring. Satisfied clients are often willing to recommend your services to friends and family if incentivized. Here's how to encourage referrals:
- Referral Rewards: Offer a discount or gift card to clients who refer new business to you. This reward motivates clients to spread the word.
- Publicize the Program: Make sure clients know about your referral program by mentioning it in emails, follow-ups, and on your website.
- Thanking Clients for Referrals: Send a personalized thank-you note or small gift to clients who refer others, reinforcing their value to your business.

Encouraging referrals is a way to organically expand your client base while deepening relationships with existing clients. A solid referral system benefits both clients and your business.

By focusing on loyalty programs, consistent follow-ups, and an effective referral system, your flooring business can create lasting client relationships that drive long-term growth and success. These approaches not only differentiate your business but also increase the likelihood that clients will choose your services over those of your competitors.

Leveraging Your Strengths

In a crowded market, understanding and maximizing your strengths can give your flooring business a powerful edge. This section covers how to highlight your team's expertise, market your commitment to quality, and use client testimonials to build credibility and attract more clients.

Highlighting Team Expertise and Experience

Your team's skills and experience are key assets that can set you apart. When potential clients know they're working with knowledgeable, skilled professionals, they're more likely to choose your business over competitors. Here's how to highlight your team's expertise:
- Showcase Certifications and Training: If your team members have certifications in flooring installation, design, or repair, make sure to highlight this on your website and marketing materials.
- Feature Team Members on Your Website: Including profiles and photos of your team members with details on their experience builds trust and personalizes your brand.
- Share Team Success Stories: Showcase successful projects that demonstrate the skill and dedication of your team. This also gives clients insight into the quality of your work.

Communicating your team's expertise helps clients feel confident in choosing your business, especially for complex or high-end projects.

Showcasing Quality and Reliability in Marketing

Quality and reliability are crucial factors for clients when choosing a flooring provider. Here's how to market these attributes effectively:
- Highlight Quality Assurance Processes: Outline the quality control measures you take to ensure every project meets high standards. Whether it's material selection, installation techniques, or inspections, clients appreciate transparency about quality.
- Promote Your Warranty or Service Guarantees: If you offer warranties on your installations or a satisfaction guarantee, make this known. A warranty provides clients with peace of mind and reinforces your commitment to quality.
- Use Professional Imagery: Invest in high-quality photos of completed projects to display on your website and social media. Showcasing your work visually communicates your commitment to excellence.

Positioning your business as a reliable, high-quality service provider attracts clients who value long-lasting, expertly installed flooring solutions.

Using Client Testimonials and Success Stories

Client testimonials are a powerful way to build credibility. Potential clients are often influenced by the experiences of others, so showcasing positive feedback can make your business stand out. Here's how to leverage testimonials effectively:
- Display Testimonials Prominently on Your Website: Use a dedicated section on your website for client testimonials, focusing on detailed feedback that highlights your strengths.
- Include Success Stories with Photos: When possible, add before-and-after photos to accompany testimonials. Visuals make client feedback more impactful and engaging.
- Share Positive Reviews on Social Media: Highlight glowing reviews or successful project stories on social media platforms to reach a wider audience.

Client testimonials and success stories reinforce the value of your services and build trust with new clients, making them more likely to choose your business over competitors.

By leveraging your team's expertise, promoting quality and reliability, and showcasing client testimonials, your flooring business can establish a reputation as a trusted, high-quality provider. These strategies not only help differentiate your business but also attract clients who value professionalism and excellence in their flooring projects.

Innovating to Stay Ahead

In a constantly evolving market, innovation is essential for maintaining a competitive edge. By adopting new technologies, exploring eco-friendly materials, and offering custom solutions, your flooring business can continue attracting clients and staying relevant. This section covers ways to use innovation as a strategy to differentiate your services and appeal to a modern, forward-thinking clientele.

Staying Updated on Industry Trends

The flooring industry, like many others, evolves regularly with new materials, techniques, and consumer preferences. Staying current with these trends positions your business as modern and adaptable. Here's how to keep up:
- Follow Industry Publications and News Sources: Trade magazines, blogs, and industry newsletters provide insights on the latest materials, technology, and design trends.
- Attend Trade Shows and Conferences: Industry events offer a first-hand look at the latest flooring innovations, from high-tech tools to sustainable products.
- Engage in Professional Development: Participating in workshops, webinars, and training programs ensures you're familiar with the latest techniques and best practices.

Clients are often drawn to businesses that stay ahead of the curve, making trend awareness a valuable asset for staying competitive.

Offering Custom Solutions

Custom solutions allow clients to tailor flooring choices to their unique needs and preferences. This level of personalization not only appeals to clients but also sets your business apart from competitors offering standard options. Here are ways to integrate custom solutions:
- Personalized Design Consultations: Offer consultations where clients can discuss their specific preferences, such as patterns, colors, or layouts, with a designer or expert.
- Custom Flooring Options: Provide exclusive designs, inlays, or custom color selections for clients looking for one-of-a-kind flooring solutions.
- Adaptable Installation Techniques: Invest in tools and techniques that allow for flexibility during installation, giving clients more choices in terms of layout and finish.

Custom services create a unique client experience, making your business memorable and increasing the likelihood of client referrals.

Exploring Eco-Friendly and Sustainable Flooring Options

With the growing focus on sustainability, many clients seek eco-friendly flooring options. Offering sustainable products not only appeals to this environmentally-conscious market but also builds a positive reputation. Here's how to incorporate sustainability:
- Offer Green Flooring Materials: Include options such as bamboo, cork, and reclaimed wood, which are sustainable and environmentally friendly.
- Highlight Low-VOC and Non-Toxic Products: Many clients are interested in products that don't release harmful chemicals. Emphasize non-toxic adhesives, finishes, and materials.
- Showcase Sustainable Practices in Marketing: Let clients know about your sustainable practices, from recycling materials to minimizing waste on job sites.

Sustainability can be a powerful differentiator, attracting clients who value eco-consciousness and supporting a positive brand image.

Investing in Technology and Tools

Advancements in flooring technology can improve efficiency, precision, and client satisfaction. Embracing new tools and techniques allows your business to work faster and achieve higher-quality results. Consider the following:
- Digital Measurement and Layout Tools: Tools like laser measurements or digital layout software improve accuracy and save time, especially on large or complex projects.
- High-Tech Installation Equipment: Investing in modern installation equipment can lead to smoother finishes and more durable installations.
- Online Design Simulators for Clients: Some flooring businesses offer online tools where clients can visualize different flooring options in their own space. This tool helps clients feel more confident in their choices.

By investing in innovation, you're not only making your business more efficient but also providing a higher level of service that stands out from competitors.

By staying updated on trends, offering custom solutions, promoting eco-friendly options, and investing in technology, your flooring business can remain competitive and appealing to clients seeking high-quality, modern services. Innovation is the key to keeping your business relevant and thriving, even in a crowded market.

Chapter 10: Looking Ahead to Continued Success

Reflecting on Your Journey and Accomplishments

Starting a flooring business is a significant accomplishment, one that requires vision, planning, and perseverance. As you've moved through each phase, from laying the foundation of your business to developing strong client relationships and refining operations, you've built not just a business but a brand rooted in quality, reliability, and integrity. Reflect on each milestone, whether big or small, and remember that each accomplishment contributes to a greater journey.

Building a Business from the Ground Up

Your journey started with a vision, which you've transformed into a thriving enterprise. Every goal you've reached, from gaining your first client to managing larger projects, is a testament to your commitment. Recognize the growth that has occurred, not only in the business but also in your capabilities as an entrepreneur. Celebrate these wins—they are well-earned markers of your progress and promise of future achievements.

Adapting and Learning Along the Way

One of the most valuable aspects of this journey has been learning through each experience. Each project, challenge, and success has contributed to a growing body of knowledge that will continue to guide your business decisions. The lessons learned—whether in client relations, financial management, or operational efficiency—prepare you to adapt to future opportunities and challenges with confidence.

Building Confidence in Your Vision

As you look back on the skills you've developed and the relationships you've built, know that you're positioned to move forward with a clear, confident vision for your business. Trust in the foundation you've created, and carry forward the belief that your hard work and resilience will continue to yield rewards.

Embracing Growth and Adaptability

The flooring industry, like many others, is continually evolving with new technologies, materials, and client expectations. Embracing change and being willing to adapt are essential traits for sustaining long-term success. Growth comes not just from expansion but from an openness to learn, adapt, and refine your business practices to meet the changing needs of clients and the market.

Staying Responsive to Industry Trends

Keeping up with industry trends allows your business to remain competitive and offer clients the latest innovations. Here's how to stay informed and responsive:

1. Follow Flooring Industry News and Innovations
2. Attend Industry Conferences and Trade Shows
3. Invest in Training for New Techniques or Products
4. Survey Clients About Emerging Preferences

Refining Business Practices for Efficiency

Streamlining business practices enhances productivity, reduces costs, and allows more time for growth-focused activities.

Expanding Services Based on Client Needs

Adapting your service offerings to meet client needs allows your business to grow and remain relevant.

Building a Legacy of Quality and Service

Building a lasting legacy in the flooring industry goes beyond profits; it's about establishing a reputation for quality, reliability, and ethical practices. A legacy business stands the test of time by prioritizing long-term relationships, client satisfaction, and excellence in service.

Focusing on Quality and Craftsmanship
Creating a Client-Centered Service Model
Leaving a Positive Impact on the Community
Creating a Legacy Through Ethical Practices

The Power of Networking and Community Involvement

Establishing connections within your industry and community can significantly impact the growth and resilience of your business.

Building a Strong Industry Network
Nurturing Local Community Relationships
Maximizing Client Referrals Through Community Engagement
Fostering a Reputation as a Community Leader

Final Words of Encouragement

As you close this guide and embark on the next phase of your business journey, remember that success in the flooring industry is built on hard work, resilience, and a commitment to excellence.

Celebrate Every Milestone

Stay Focused on Your Vision
Embrace Lifelong Learning
Value Relationships and Community
Believe in Your Ability to Succeed

As you look ahead, know that your journey is just beginning. With a commitment to quality, a focus on client satisfaction, and a passion for your craft, you're well-prepared for the challenges and triumphs ahead. Here's to your continued success, growth, and fulfillment in building a flooring business that stands the test of time.

www.ingramcontent.com/pod-product-compliance
Lightning Source LLC
Chambersburg PA
CBHW071403210526

45465CB00001B/232